Coming Forth as Gold

Coming Forth as Gold

Where Seeds Are Transformed in the Dark

ADELE CHARLES

Coming Forth As Gold: Where Seeds Are Transformed in the Dark
Published by Unveil Her Harvest

Author's Note
The events depicted in this book are authentic, and the people are real. The names and some places have been changed out of respect for privacy. All conversations are real and have been reconstructed to the best of my knowledge. All court discussions are drawn from actual court transcripts I purchased, which are public records.

Library of Congress Control Number: 2026904016

ISBN: 979-8-90252-044-3 (Paperback)
ISBN: 979-8-90252-045-0 (eBook)

For Ya Ya, – you always believed in me
and left a beautiful legacy

For my children, Reece, Kingston and Scarlett
God is using your birth and lives for His glory

Job 23:10 NIV
"But He knows the way that I take;
when He has tested me,
-
I will come forth as gold."

Table of Contents

Coming Forth As Gold
Where Seeds Are Transformed in the Dark

"We are pressed on every side by troubles but
not crushed and broken.
We are perplexed because we don't know why things
happen the way they do,
But we don't give up and quit. We are hunted down, but
God never abandons us.
We get knocked down, but we get up again and
keep going."
2 Corinthians 4: 8 – 9
Life Application Bible for Students

I GET UP. I WALK. I FALL DOWN.
MEANWHILE
I KEEP DANCIING.
- Unknown

Beginning My Career

As soon as graduation ended in 2009, the search for my dream-teaching career began. As the economy continued to struggle and the market fell downward, teaching jobs in Colorado were far and few between. But as life often throws a curveball, and I had seen quite a few in my life; this was not going to get me down. I knew that walking into this game of searching for a job and sending out my resume was only going to get an employer's attention if I knew them personally or if I had worked in their district. I must have sent out and personally hand delivered more than fifty resumes and cover letters, yet not once did I receive a call back or an invitation for an interview. I couldn't figure this out. I had left the university at the top of my class, being told I was to be snatched up by the first principal I came across, but this was not the case.

I began to get burned out as this job search was going nowhere almost a month after my graduation on May 9, 2009, I began to think, how could I get this far and not get the career I always dreamed of?

But God knew the desires of my heart, and He knew what I had always wanted. I had this dream of teaching overseas, living somewhere tropical, and all of my college classmates knew this. Yet, I didn't think I could quite teach overseas just yet, as Akuma would need to work on his U.S.

residency and later citizenship, so teaching overseas wasn't an option, or was it?

Being bent up about not having a career right after graduation led to many sleepless nights of searching on the internet, updating my cover letters, and emailing friends here and there.

On one particular evening, I was up until three in the morning playing around on Facebook when I came across a familiar face I had known long ago in my early college days. I befriended her and discovered she worked in the United States Virgin Islands. I was awestruck by this and had to find out more. I discovered she worked for an independent school on St. Thomas. This engrossed me so much, that I investigated a bit more, only to find myself sending my resume, some lesson plans I created, a few pictures of a particular lesson and a brief email to the headmaster. I went to bed laughing at myself, thinking, "Did I just apply to work at a school in the U.S. Virgin Islands?"

I woke up early to find an email the headmaster sent me saying he enjoyed what I sent and mentioned my information was forwarded to the principal, Magliana Casoria, on campus.

I was in utter disbelief, for this was the first response I had received all month from any school, let alone a school in the Caribbean.

That same morning I was leisurely enjoying my day off when I received a phone call from the area code 340. Where was 340 from? To my surprise, it was the area code for the U.S. Virgin Islands, and Magliana Casoria, the principal, was on the other end. I was taken aback and was left almost speechless as to how quickly everything was forming.

"Good afternoon, may I speak with Adele?" inquired Ms. Casoria.

"Oh, this is she. May I ask who is calling?" I nervously responded.

"Good day, this is Magliana Casoria. I am the principal of Frenchman's Bay School in the U.S. Virgin Islands," she responded boldly.

"Oh, wow. It's so wonderful to hear from you. Wow. How are you? I have so many questions I wanted to ask you about Frenchman's Bay. I am currently out and not at my office. Would there be another chance for us to speak further when I return home?" I stated with excitement.

"Yes, that would be fine. I look forward to connecting with you soon," she stated.

I hung up and screamed with enthusiasm.

Was this happening? Seriously?

I sent out countless emails to principals throughout the metropolitan area, hand-delivered cover letters and resumes to various schools, and finally, to my surprise, the dream school I stayed up for in the early morning hours, cranking out my passionate work and best teaching practices, had not only seen my work, but commented on it, and it had been passed on to several of the headmaster's colleagues on campus. I was dumbfounded and incredibly grateful.

Over the following week and a half, I spent time researching the island of St. Thomas, sharing my thoughts, my teaching philosophy, and my desire to become a teacher at this school. Within the first twelve days of June, I was offered a position teaching middle school on the island.

Finally, a thought occurred to me. This was the United States. It was a territory of the United States, and with that, Akuma could continue to work on his U.S. residency and later citizenship, even if we moved to the U.S.V.I.. After much thought, prayer, and consideration, Akuma and I began looking for a place to live in STT, St. Thomas.

Within two months, we had sold all of our winter wool sweaters (whoop whoop!), our car, and had six bags packed on a red-eye flight to STT.

The Unfolding of His Beauty

Early in the month of August, we arrived mid-afternoon in sunny St. Thomas. Everyone around us on our flight was excited for their summer vacation, their honeymoons or weekend getaways, while I quietly realized I was moving to this paradise that many from all over the world were only visiting.

We deplaned, gathered our life from the conveyer belt, and began our journey into this exotic destination, observing our driver navigate the left side of the road. Everything about this place was different from anything I knew or was used to; yet I knew this was God's gift to me, as I had always dreamed of teaching somewhere outside of the state of Colorado.

We settled into a studio condo on the north side of the island overlooking Mahogany Run golf course. Our first night on the island was spent outside on our balcony, overlooking the green fairways and valley facing the Caribbean Sea. As dusk descended, the fluffy jet-puffed clouds turned exuberant shades of colors as the sun disappeared for the day.

Later that evening, everything that had happened from that day began to sink in as I reflected on this precise place God had set out for me, knowing this is where he wanted me to be. Everything from the night before and that evening seemed surreal to me.

Had God really known me this well? Had He known the desires of my heart? He surely had, and even though I thought at times He had forgotten about me, gazing up into the starry night sky I knew I was loved unconditionally.

Waking up the following morning to the warm sunshine and distinctive tropical décor stirred my senses. I stood with my favorite cup of Jamaican coffee out on the warm-tiled balcony, only to spot four to five green parrots chasing each other in and out of the mahogany trees below.

The first ten days of living on St. Thomas were spent getting to know the island, getting familiar with the West Indian culture, and enjoying His beauty. Not only had I embarked on beginning my teaching career, but I had been hand-picked by the man upstairs into a serene landscape filled with wonder and splendor.

Our first trip to the beach was to Magen's Bay, just five minutes from our new bungalow. The waters of the bay took my breath away. I had never seen waters so undisturbed, fresh, clear, and blue. Walking across the soft sand, my feet and toes waltzed to the music of the soft waves that brushed up against the shore of the bay. Everywhere I walked, and everything my eyes were fixed upon, revealed a glimpse of God's beauty and of His love for me.

I woke up every day in awe of where I lived. Some days I knew exactly where I was, but most of the time I couldn't believe God had loved me so much to put me in a place as beautiful as the Virgin Islands.

Island Vibes

The campus where I taught was absolutely beautiful. It was a large campus that served students from preschool to the twelfth grade. It sat on the southern part of the island, nestled near Havensight, one of the island's world-class ports of entrance.

I remember the first week of work well. Driving on the left side was such a rush and adventure. The roads were small and incredibly windy. So many of the roads reminded me of Lombard Street in San Francisco. At most, the top speed was thirty-five miles per hour, so traveling at a high rate of speed was never an option, let alone recommended. I recall thinking to myself several times while driving up and down steep island roads, "Man, if it ever snowed here, we would be doomed. There is no way I could drive on this road in the snow."

Getting adjusted to island style living was entertaining, to say the least. Most of the islanders knew when the "fresh meat" arrived on island, and I was a walking example of one. I stood at the busy intersection on Raphune Hill in front of Tutu Park Mall for several minutes trying to figure out when to cross the street.

A Safari bus driver yelled out his window, "NOW, GO NOW! You can cross the street." Wisdom and kindness were given all at once.

Many of the inhabitants of the Virgin Islands were extremely helpful individuals and took their time with you as you adapted to their culture. The West Indian flair and culture were colorful, artistic, and wonderfully unique.

Room 309

Work week had arrived, and I was formally introduced to the faculty of the school. I stood with confidence as I began my first day as a middle school reading – language arts and geography – ancient civilizations teacher at Frenchman's Bay School in St. Thomas, U.S.V.I.. With my classroom keys in hand, I opened the door to classroom 309 where eighteen desks were placed to fill the minds of my first class of thirty-six students.

I loved my classroom. It had these huge floor-to-ceiling windows that could have been considered open – air. Yet, after weeks of teaching, I discovered I had a bit of a wild iguana and chicken problem during my students' morning break and lunch break hours.

One of many things I treasured about my first-year teaching on island was how exceptionally diverse my school and classroom were. Within the first group of thirty-six middle schoolers I taught – thirty-two of my students represented different ethnic backgrounds, various countries, and multiple religious backgrounds. What stood out to me from day one – was how accepting the student body and faculty were in supporting one another. I had never experienced such an aesthetic adornment of excellence in my teaching background until then.

My first year teaching at this school was challenging yet rewarding. The dynamics of teaching a diverse learning audience from all over the West Indies, and students whose backgrounds came from all parts of the world, were a new learning experience that I will always hold close to my heart.

Some of the best memories occurred during those years in classroom 309, and I will fondly remember it all for the remainder of my life. My first class of students held high expectations of me and left my class as amazing writers and incredible community leaders on our island as the years progressed in their school careers. I finished that year feeling accomplished for completing the curriculum I dove into, poured my passion into, and taught with love.

Summer 2010

During my first summer on the island, I had a conversation with my husband about my desire to start a family. We had an in-depth conversation about it and decided we would begin our journey of trying to get pregnant. I bought a few books on pregnancy, a book on baby names, and a few others to get started.

I was thrilled to embark on this next milestone in my life. My dream to become a mother was right up there with my current career. I always dreamt of the adventure of motherhood as a child. I grew up loving kids and studied at the university to fulfill a profound career educating children to help them learn and achieve their dreams.

I envisioned for many years having a boy named Reece. I had always loved this name, and I would often joke with Akuma, "Oh, I can't wait to see what Reece looks like. I can see him running around, laughing, and running into my arms."

The thought of becoming pregnant was fun and enjoyable and I believed that we would get pregnant right away, even by accident, from what had happened with so many of my friends.

Nevertheless, we continued on our trek to become parents, and our journey into parenthood took us into my second year of teaching at Frenchman's Bay School.

Fall 2010 – Spring 2011

Akuma and I continued to work on becoming pregnant. Our journey began in July of 2010 and continued from one month into the next, and into the next. It continued into a miserable trend. Nothing was happening, and I began to feel discouraged and depressed.

The activity of trying began to become a task; having intercourse at this point became mundane and somewhat horrendous. It wasn't fun anymore.

Creating a life inside my womb was not easy to accomplish. Every month, I was hopeful my period would be late, but I always ended up starting my menstrual cycle. Every time I started my cycle, I would cry. Every month, tears were shed. I began to wonder how difficult this could be when so many of my friends around me were pregnant; some weren't even trying, and they were able to create their baby bump. I finished up my second year of teaching feeling personally defeated.

Why was this so difficult? Why couldn't we get pregnant?

When your Dreams Keep Testing Negative

One year had passed since the now taxing desire to become pregnant – an entire year, 365 days of sorrow and heartbreak. One unsuccessful attempt after another was devastating to my psyche. How could this dream of mine be so untouchable? Those books I had purchased on baby names and what to expect when expecting were tossed into the back of my closet. My dreams seemed to be fading away.

I was determined to figure this out, so I began to do some serious research on what it takes to become pregnant. Through my research, these questions were consistent – Was I ovulating on time? Was my cycle normal? How thick or thin was my cervical mucus? What was my temperature during ovulation? Was I having intercourse at the right time? Was I having intercourse often enough? What does it take to become pregnant?

These questions were constantly running through my head day in and day out. It seemed as if the days were getting longer. Every waking second, I lived and breathed these questions and ***every time*** I continued to get my monthly cycle.

WHAT DOES IT TAKE?!?

I became more and more frustrated and angry as time passed. It was challenging, especially when friends of mine were getting pregnant without even trying, while on birth control, or it only took one time, and they were fertile "myrtle".

The more I researched, the more it seemed like my chances of conceiving were a stagnant dream. One where I could only imagine having children, let alone just one child, and it would never become *my* reality.

Throughout my second teaching year on the island, I had been in contact with my primary care doctor back home in Colorado. We had discussed various things to try, and it became evident to my doctor that I needed to attend another level of care to see if I could achieve my dream of conceiving.

Many primary care doctors suggest getting further testing and going to a specialty clinic to try other avenues of achieving a positive pregnancy test. That summer, I returned home for further testing with a women's clinic that specialized in obstetrics, gynecology and hormone therapy.

My first appointment at the women's clinic occurred on August 4, 2011. It was to cover a routine pap smear to see if anything was abnormal there. I was asked to do some blood work to determine if I was considered to have an Advanced Maternal Age, AMA, by checking my Thyroid-stimulating hormone, or TSH, and Prolactin to be able to diagnose the cause of infertility.

I had another appointment set at the clinic a week and a half later to perform a follicle check and screening on August 15th. The doctor had given me a 2D ultrasound to take measurements of my uterus and both of my ovaries, as well as check my trilaminar endometrial lining, cervix, adnexae, Cul de sac, and bladder. The 2D screening was negative, and there was no free fluid. My results for TSH and Prolactin were both in range. My pap smear came back normal.

At this time, I was thirty-two years old. I discovered my progesterone levels were low, and we were working on trying to determine if I could get pregnant or not. I couldn't proceed with further testing, as I was getting ready to head back to the island within the next six days for my third year at Frenchman's Bay School.

The fact that some of the tests came back normal according to where I was on my cycle day left me feeling hopeful that something positive would transpire in the months to come.

Transitions

I started my winter break from Frenchman's Bay sooner so I could travel back to Colorado to undergo a test called a Hysterosalpingogram, or HSG test. This test had to be performed between day 4 and 12 of my menstrual cycle.

This test was performed at a world-renowned fertility clinic known as the Colorado Center of Reproductive Medicine, or CCRM. I chose this clinic because it's famous for its high success rates of conception and live births. I knew going into this I was in great hands with the many fertility doctors who would soon have an impact on my journey to conceive.

The HSG test was performed in a radiology suite, and dye was injected to assess my fallopian tubes to see if they were open and to check if my uterine cavity was normal. I received the results, and everything came back open and normal, so the questions about why I couldn't conceive continued.

During my Christmas break, I returned to the specialist at a local women's clinic. The doctor scheduled an Intrauterine Insemination, or IUI. I was pulling out all the stops during my holiday recess from teaching to work on achieving my dream of a positive pregnancy test. I had high hopes of pregnancy once I knew the HSG test went well, as I was taking all the right steps to ensure sure the sperm got to where it needed to be by having that doctor execute the IUI.

I returned to the island, got back into my teaching groove, and discovered that the sperm and egg never met. I was once again disappointed with yet another menstrual cycle.

Teaching day in and day out, month after month, began to take a toll on my emotions. I walked into my classroom, inspiring those who sat at the desks in room 309, and went home feeling defeated by my biggest aspiration of becoming the mom I dreamed to be. I began to get depressed and felt completely hopeless. I never imagined this would be so difficult, and to come to terms, I was the one suffering from it. I gained a lot of weight as I emotionally ate during the second semester of teaching; my emotions got a hold of me, and I wasn't willing to continue my dream teaching career in a destination I absolutely loved, working on the island, with my desire of a positive pregnancy test slipping away.

The hope and dream of becoming a mom began to fade away with each passing month and year.

I kept thinking, "Gosh, my biological clock is ticking, and I'm getting older; NOTHING is happening. What if this is my only chance to become a mom?" I contemplated so many things.

So much of me loved what I had done in my career on St. Thomas: the families and students I taught who had such a positive impact on my life, the colleagues I had grown to love and considered my closest friends, and the island home and culture I treasured so much.

My mind would go back and forth as I continued to ask questions – What if I am not supposed to have kids? What if moving off the island is a mistake? How can I leave the career I love and adore? How can I leave St. Thomas?

I went through this dilemma all throughout my final year on the island and decided this was my one shot at becoming a mom. I was willing to risk everything to achieve that goal, so in March of 2012, I notified my headmaster, principal, my basketball team I coached for three years, and all of my students whom I had grown to love and respect that this would be my final year teaching on the island.

Only a few trusted colleagues knew why I made plans to leave the school I loved. They knew my heart ached as I wanted to know what it was like to carry a child, and they knew this was my one opportunity to achieve my dream.

I remember my last few days on the island; I took a ferry to St. John to have one last hurrah at my favorite spot – Cinnamon Bay. I stared off into the distance of St. John as the car ferry left the dock in Red Hook. I allowed the warm Caribbean breeze to sweep across my face as the sunlight danced upon the ripples of the ocean below the boat. I pondered what my future would hold as I thought about what would happen next.

The memories of the past three years sat heavy with me as I sat at Cinnamon Bay, gazing off onto the Caribbean blue waves that gently hugged the sand and my toes on that warm morning. I wanted to soak in all the goodness I had those years on the shores of the Virgin Islands.

Some of my favorite memories on the island included the following: buying books written by Caribbean authors from the Dockside Bookstore in Havensight; the greetings of "Goo mahrin, goo aftanoon, and goo night," something I still embrace to this day; limin' with great friends at Lindquist, boat trips to Jost, Tola, and Virgin Gorda. Sunset sails with the Ritz Carlton's late Lady Lynsey; car ferries to St. John; snorkeling at Coki Beach and Trunk Bay; flavored mojitos at Morning Star beach; lunch breaks at Barefoot Buddha. Enjoying happy hour and amazing hamburgers at Shipwrecked Tavern; avoiding cruise traffic at the end of a teaching day; Miracle on Mainstreet; the Danish architecture; steel pan, Cultural Food Fair, J'Ouvet, farmer's market in Yacht Haven Grand; opening night in Carnival

Village; painkillers, Paradise Point, breadfruit, bush tea, guava berry rum sold on the side of the road at Fredericks ballpark; getting gas at GasWorks; pizza and wings at Island Time Pub; nights out at Duffy's Love Shack; writing lesson plans at Sapphire Beach; watching the seaplanes land in the harbor; listening to the cruise ships as they entered the Havensight port; dinner at Rancho Latino; the ambiance of Havana Blue; happy hour with my colleagues at Iggie's; Christmas Staff parties at amazing villas; breakfast at the Delly Deck; shopping at the Fruit Bowl, Gourmet Gallery, the Food Center, Plaza Extra; ice cream and rum at Udder Delight after a day at Magen's Bay, purchasing snacks and wine at Starfish Market; the best lamb gyros at Aqua Bistro; donkeys roaming St. John; Annaberg Sugar Plantation, soaking up the sun at Cinnamon Bay; riding in a Safari bus for field trips; the Quadrille Dancers who dance to Quelbe music; stopping roadside to pick genip; Vienna cake for special occasions; homemade passion fruit juice; driving to Drake's Seat to watch the sunset; #positiveishowILive, #VItilIDie, Rock City, Brewer's Bay to watch the planes land on the rock; Paradise Jam, JamBand, hot Johnny Cake at many of the booths during Carnival; watching rainbows and rain showers over the Caribbean Sea; Morgan's Mango with wonderful friends; shopping for unique jewelry on Main Street; Caribbean Hook bracelets and listening to live music in Frenchtown at Rum Shandy's.

These were many of the activities I enjoyed throughout my three years there – so many wonderful memories, too many to write about. I enjoyed my last soak in St. John, remembering some firsts with lifelong friends and colleagues who welcomed me to the school where I taught and fell in love with the West Indian culture. One of my colleagues, originally from Argentina, invited some colleagues over to her home in Mandahl Bay for evening cocktails and a wonderful gathering. During the Christmas holiday, she gifted us with a Caribbean cookbook and homemade rum cake.

A wonderful couple I had the pleasure of working with and getting to know rather well -- a local author and his beautiful, artistic wife. I enjoyed the pleasure of getting to know this amazing couple, well-versed and loved by many on the island. They invited us over to their treetop bungalow on the north side of the island for hors d'oeuvres and afterwards took us down to Carnival Village for opening night, live Soca, dancehall music, carnival rides, johnny cake, drinks, and a great time together.

I spent the afternoon soaking up my last bit of my favorite place to lime and took the evening ferry back to St. Thomas. The starry night out on the Caribbean Sea would have to meet me at another time and place.

Fall 2012

Returning to the United States was a bit of a culture shock for me; it took about six months before I felt like

I was at home again. I had left the culture of the island behind, along with my dream career. Being in Colorado was a challenge. I left the island without a job offer and began my search in Denver. I was unable to find a full-time teaching position, and it was completely frustrating. So much seemed to be falling apart in my opinion – no career, no pregnancy, no kids. I began to feel like I had no purpose.

My precious grandmother, Ya Ya, was sweet enough to offer to help me, saying she would pay me to take her to the grocery store, her never-ending doctor's appointments, and to clean her house. I was grateful for her ability to make me feel like I had purpose during this difficult time. What I loved about helping her the most was being able to learn from her and to spend quality time with her. We gained an incredible friendship during this difficult season, and I will forever be grateful for her encouraging words, kind heart, and generous spirit.

A few months into the fall, I was able to find some work by becoming a substitute teacher for one of the largest school districts, taking a tutoring job teaching a few students English and grammar on the side, and continuing to help and support my grandmother, Ya Ya, throughout the week.

I continued to go months into the fall with more disappointment from negative pregnancy tests. I refused to read any more books about getting pregnant and I became more and more depressed.

Questions would rise up – "Why did I leave the island? Why did I move here? Why can't I get pregnant?"

I vividly remember driving home from my grandmother's house and getting off my exit to return home – gripping my steering wheel, looking up, and yelling at God – "IS THIS ALL I AM WORTH? WHY CAN'T I GET PREGNANT? WHY CAN'T I GET A FULL TIME TEACHING POSITION?" I became more and more angry and frustrated in my disappointments and lack of purpose in my drive to do the things I loved and dreamt of becoming. Having to go to specialists for the concept of getting pregnant was weighing on my heart and mind.

January 2013

In early January, my specialist told me to go get an AMH blood test. AMH stands for Anti-mullerian hormones. The AMH plays an important role in reproduction, as it is the very best test to check the ovarian reserve. Depending on the levels of your AMH, it will detect how many eggs you have or if you are on the brink of menopause. I was informed that to be a candidate for IVF, my AMH level needed to be between one and three.

On January 12th, I went to a clinic to get the AMH test. I felt hopeful, thinking I was young enough to believe that conceiving on my own was a possibility. A week later, I received my results; my AMH score was 0.9. Shortly after receiving my results, a nurse practitioner called me and discussed my score with me.

"Hi, Adele, this is Kathy from the women's clinic. I wanted to go over the results of your AMH score. After looking through your test results, it is in my highest recommendation that you and your husband consider in-vitro fertilization. I don't believe it will be possible to conceive on your own," she stated.

I immediately hung up the phone and began sobbing. My emotions were high, and I felt a deep heartache within my chest. It was like the floor shifted beneath me the moment the words left my doctor's mouth: "Your only option is IVF." The sentence hung in the air – heavy, final, like a door slamming shut on every quiet dream I had of conceiving naturally. The vision I carried for years – seeing two lines on a test, surprising Akuma, feeling life spark inside me – suddenly felt stolen.

It's not just disappointment; it's grief.

It's the sinking weight that settles in my stomach, pulling me down as I question – what's wrong with me? Why can't my body do what it's supposed to do?

The envy of others' easy pregnancies flashed sharply.

I will never have my **own** child. How can this be? Out of everyone in my family, I was the one who saw myself with a family, lots of kids, lots of love…my dream is gone. This one test is telling me I will never get pregnant. I will **NEVER** be able to afford IVF. Why is this happening to me? Why me?

My mom was in the next room and came running in to figure out what was going on.

"Adele, oh my Del, what is wrong? Why are you so upset?" she asked worriedly.

"Mom, she said I would never conceive on my own. The IUI will never work and she wants me to look into IVF. I can't afford IVF. I will never become a mom! I will never achieve my dream. This makes me so, so heartsore. It hurts so deeply," I wept uncontrollably.

My mom left the other room for some time and came back to sit with me on the couch.

"Adele, I spoke with Ya Ya on the phone and we have decided that we will help you pay for IVF," my mom kindly shared.

"No, Mom, I cannot let you do this for me. I just won't. You have been a single mother for so long and I don't want to be the one responsible for taking away some of your retirement money to live off of. That's not fair to you and it's not fair to Ya Ya to do this for me," I replied despairingly.

"Adele, my sweet daughter, this is your dream. I know it is because it's affected you so deeply; and to be honest, it's just money. Your dream to become a mother is more important than money. We would like to help you do this. Ya Ya and I are willing to pitch in $20,000 each. Let's go ahead and call CCRM and schedule a consultation with one of the best doctors they have."

I cried heavy tears of gratitude and began looking up the phone number for Colorado Center of Reproductive Medicine. I called and explained the referral from my specialist to the personnel at the front desk and asked to schedule a consultation with the doctor who has been known to have many successes with patients who have struggled with infertility for over 30 years. He is the one I chose to be my infertility doctor.

"Good afternoon, I would like to schedule a consultation for in-vitro fertilization? How soon can I be seen?" I nervously requested.

"Good afternoon, let me pull up his schedule and I will get right back with you…okay, Adele… are you there? He has an opening at 12:15pm on Monday, April 22nd. Does this work for you?" she quickly informed me.

"Uh, yeah, April 22nd will work," I replied. Wow, three months out? That far away from now, hmmm, he must be a very good doctor, I thought.

"Great, Adele, let me gather all of your information and I will get you set up for the 22nd. In the meantime, have you heard about our exclusive support group for CCRM? We have a few locations. One is mid-month at our Rose Hospital location in Denver from 10 a.m. to 11:30 a.m., and another one is at the beginning of the month, here at our Lone Tree office from 1 p.m. – 2:30 p.m. These sessions are open to all clients of CCRM and they occur on Saturdays at those locations and times. You are welcome to come as a couple or on your own."

"Great, thank you so much. I will start attending them. I definitely could use some encouragement during this time. Thank you for your help, have a wonderful day. Goodbye," I said gratefully.

Towards the end of the month, my mental health began to decline. The infertility had taken its toll on me. I had scheduled an appointment with my favorite family doctor and she prescribed me an anti-depressant to take the edge off of the emotional and mental effects of infertility. My thoughts were all over the place and my life seemed empty. The anti-depressant brought a sense of calm and helped me relax more.

Three Months Until April 22, 2013

The first few weeks of February, I had begun the anti-depressant and had several job interviews that ended up being a dead end.

My sweet grandmother Ya Ya, who was aging beautifully at age eighty-six, needed more one-on-one assistance. Most of the family had full schedules and busy lives and were unable to care for Ya Ya, so I took the initiative of caring for and tending to my grandmother's weekly needs for doctor and salon appointments, as well as grocery store runs. Our time together in my in-betweens is something

I still treasure to this day. We were going through various changes in our own lives. Two generations of women, one growing gracefully and me, waiting in hope of dreams to be conceived.

I took advantage of joining the first CCRM support care group on February 16th at Rose Medical Center. I met the CCRM's counselor in a quiet office space with fresh fruit, Fage plain yogurt, and water. Other women and a few couples trickled in as we began to form a circle with the chairs in the waiting room.

The room's ambience felt dry, heavy, and emotional as many others like me sat in their own grief and sadness wondering when, why, and if it was possible for them, and for us.

So many unanswered questions, intense emotions, and memories of loss, frustration, and defeat were felt and seen as we wept, shared our stories, and began to understand we weren't in this battle alone. Someone like me was going through much of the same feelings, experiences, and processes.

I attended an additional five support group sessions throughout those three months and began looking forward to my time spent there. One of the discussions the counselor shared with many of us, which continues to stick with me to this day, is the fact that all of what we were all feeling deep within our hearts and souls were marked by true sadness and deep grief. She explained to all of us that the difficulty of infertility was as evident an issue as someone dealing with terminal cancer or HIV/AIDS. This was as deep and weighty as everything I had been feeling for the past three years made sense. Infertility brought on so much grief.

So many outside of my inner circle had no clue as to what I was feeling or thinking inside. The struggle of sitting in my own solitude month after month with the disappointment of getting one menstrual cycle after another, only be thrown into a deeper depression. Going through all of the emotions, wondering if I was doing all the things right. Was my cervical mucus, right? Basal temperature? Having intercourse at the right time of day, hour, minute? Exercising enough or too much? Eating a diet that would help with my fertility? I began to question everything, even down to the minutest things. I would go from thought to thought only to feel more depressed and hopeless.

April 22, 2013

D-Day had finally arrived. The day I had been waiting for. This was either the day my life would change into dreams of promise and growth, literal growth, or years of failed realities only to be left on repeat of one loss after another.

My consultation with my doctor was rather lengthy and extremely thorough. We went over cost, treatments, the process, the work-up, procedures to add to my calendar, and everything to expect in the in-vitro journey. I was given a workbook of sorts that covered everything from A – Z for everything CCRM provided for every patient. It was my go-to for each step that I would soon be embarking on.

It was overwhelming to process all of this; so much to look at and get to know. Yet, I was eager to learn it. It was as if I was going back to school to get an education on fertility, biology, how to administer needles into my own body, and the absolute gift of life.

My doctor and I discussed the details of in-vitro and I mentioned to him that I had done one IUI in December of 2011. He mentioned the cost of doing an IUI versus IVF is a dramatically different price range. We discussed this and he wanted to give it a few more tries prior to starting IVF. The cost of an IUI was under $1000 and IVF was up in the $30,000 - $50,000 price range depending upon our situation.

I was willing to try one more IUI, a final time. I didn't want to go too far beyond that because I didn't want to waste time thinking my chances of carrying my own child and getting pregnant were on a major decline due to the AMH blood test I received a few months back. So, in late May of 2013, I completed all the work-up with medications and follicle checks, as well as getting another AMH blood test to see if this would be possible. My second IUI occurred at CCRM. I waited patiently and was trying to feel hopeful of a positive pregnancy test. It was another waiting game.

A Summer of Prayer and Deepened Heartache

Mid-June arrived and I was met with the same defeating results – I had started my period ***again***. Sitting in the quietness of the bathroom with the walls surrounding me, I began to harden my shell and my heart of ever achieving what seemed like the impossible. The coldness of sitting on the toilet seat crying out in my disappointment, a disappointment so deep I didn't think anyone or anything could cure it. The kind of pain that begins in the pit of your belly and rises into your chest; the tightness gripping at my heart and squeezing the very life out of me.

When…when…when would my dreams of motherhood begin?

I envied the women in my support group for being able to carry a child they miscarried – at least they were pregnant and were able to experience the joy of carrying their child. I couldn't even achieve this – the joy of conception. Absolutely nothing to celebrate.

Loss is all I knew, no surprises of a pregnancy stick to show off to friends and loved ones. Only a regular period every twenty-eight days, month after month, and year after year to speak of – no joys – just utter disgust that my own body was working against my heart and mind.

The results of my second IUI were defeating, as well as finding out the test results from my second AMH score in a four-month time window went from 0.9 to 0.7. I knew time was running out and my chance of ever getting pregnant on my own would be a lost cause.

How could this be? Why was this happening?

According to the medical community, I was considered young to be going through all of this. I was thirty-four and a half and my chances of conceiving my own child were slipping further and further away from me.

By mid-July, I had made it a regular habit of my first and third Saturday to attend the CCRM support group, getting regular massages, and I began acupuncture as well. My whole being was on high alert – my mental capacity was at a breaking point; my ability to get out of bed everyday became a challenge as nothing I did physically was achieving pregnancy. My physical being was strained and I needed relaxation to keep me steady when it seemed as if all around me everything was falling apart.

Intellectually, I was a student of everything involving infertility. I was hoping to read up on some new trends to achieve what I wanted and so desperately hoped for. Spiritually, I was constantly seeking and crying out to God. So much around me seemed to decay and break down.

My mom felt beside herself in my distress. She too was looking for answers and she knew I needed some kind of reassurance. She knew I was so desperate to find safety in knowing the outcome would be a positive one. She began looking and reaching out to her friends for help. She ran across a friend of hers from years ago that held a prayer-healing ministry at her house on weeknights in northwest Denver.

I figured at this point I would try anything to accomplish some peace of mind. We drove together one summer evening and pulled up to the house where many adults were waiting to get the prayer meeting started.

I introduced myself to three different women and we walked into a quiet room in the house to pray. I gave a brief synopsis of what I was going through since the summer of 2010. We sat down and each of the women laid their hands on me. I wrote down several scriptures in my Bible in pen along the margins they prayed over me with.

"Adele, I want you to look up Isaiah 54:2-3, Isaiah 55:8,9,12, Psalms 27:11, 13, 14, and Mark 11:23-24. After looking up these scriptures, I read them to the women. I was prayed over each scripture and I wrote these words in my Bible.

- Lord, thank you for healing my womb and allowing me to be fruitful. Let the words of this book speak life into my womb and soul.

- Teach me to follow. You are in control, I'm not. Thank you for giving me my child on this earth.
- Healing belongs to me. We say to this mountain of infertility – be removed.

I specifically remember one of the women praying over me and saying, "Adele, I see many children. I see a lot of children."

I couldn't help but roll my eyes and laugh. Lady, I can't even accomplish a positive pregnancy test on my own and I haven't been capable of this for over 3 years. What a joke!

September 2013

Within the first couple of weeks, I had another meeting with my doctor about my in-vitro work-up and procedures to get ready for. I already had a few procedures done in May.

This month, I would be doing a mammogram and both Akuma and I would be getting the genetic screening test done the following month.

On September 19th, I had another AMH blood test done. Going back from this past year, my first AMH blood test revealed the 0.9 result in which my former health care professional recommended finding a fertility specialist. Then, testing again in May and having my result be 0.7 – I truly believed that my results were only going to continue going further downhill with a result of 0.5, yet something incredible happened. My body reversed the medical report and my AMH score had jumped up to 2.1!

It was absolutely remarkable and jaw-dropping to think about.

Many of my friends I had gained from CCRM's fertility support groups were asking me – "Adele, what did you do differently? Did you change your diet? Exercise routine? Was it acupuncture?"

All I could say was I started to pray.

I prayed.

I prayed and God answered my prayer. I wrote about this amazing occurrence the day I received my results back on September 19, 2013. This is what I wrote –

I am overflowing with gratitude as I write…
A prayer has been answered, and I have found new hope in what is unseen.
We all feel like pebbles in the sand at some point in our lives.
Some of us sit in the hot sun for years wondering when life will give us shade.
Sometimes we are sent out to troubled waters
wondering when the sea will calm again,
and there are those of us who wish
we were a different pebble to begin with…
but if we take the time to stop reflecting on our surrounding
and look beyond the dark clouds,

you will get the chance to see glimpses of light shining
down on us.
A glimpse of light that is opening new doors of
opportunity and life.
When you take the time to glimpse the light,
You may even see a rainbow after the storm.
- Adele Charles
Thought of the Day

For the first time in years, I finally was able to grasp onto something positive from everything I was going through in my infertility journey. How in the world does my AMH score move from 0.7 to 2.1 in just four months? The only reason is – God. The Almighty God.

Shortly after this amazing miracle in my blood work, I called and asked my sister, Aster, if she had any recommendations on Bible studies to do to help me stay encouraged on this uphill struggle of achieving pregnancy, and if she would be interested in doing it with me.

Aster returned my call and suggested we do the study, "*Breaking Free: The Journey, The Stories*" by Beth Moore together. As soon as I bought this study, I knew it was going to take a lot of effort and work. It was a lengthy study with DVDs to watch and quite a bit of reading material, as well as filling in the blanks and questions to answer. This Bible study was my building block that continued to strengthen my faith and helped me to look beyond my current circumstances, no matter how many years I had been waiting for God to answer my prayers about the possibility of carrying my own child.

God had been building me in these "unknown years" to develop my character, even when I felt defeated and weak. To Christ, I was well looked after; I was His beloved daughter in whom he took great delight.

At the very beginning of this study, God started to remind me whose I was – I was His. Throughout this ten-week study, He began to plant seeds where I stumbled in knowing how much God truly loved me. God displayed His wonder in these pages as I began to grasp more of who He is and things He desired to teach me as I embarked on this upcoming IVF cycle.

Here are a few things I learned while doing this study, including small insights and deep revelations God taught me:

1. I want to rebuild some broken places. I have come for deliverance. I have come to be set free.
2. Please help me understand the sorrows I've experienced in my life. Help me understand why I always must struggle. Show me that you love me.
3. The obstacle of self-control involves the failure to trust God, a loss of hope and not being able to know God's blessings in all of this.
4. God shared this thought with me while I was doing the Bible Study – **There is a reason your**

child-to-be born has taken this long to come to be – it is for the glory of God.

5. I can now thank God for this struggle of infertility because it helped me to lean on Him and to trust Him ever more. I believe the Lord will be glorified when I do achieve pregnancy.
6. There is wisdom in obedience, Adele – continue to listen to the word of God.
7. My roots are beginning to grow. I am now standing in Christ, instead of on my own.
8. Infertility – The fact that I wanted to be in control of my life and to be able to control the outcome of becoming pregnant – it brought me to rock bottom – until I finally said, "God take it. I can't do it anymore!"
9. God desires for us to be deeply rooted in Him, so we can be a display of His splendor.
10. God wants to set us free and let us find the blessings on the other side.

God taught many things in this study; many things that would sustain me into the months ahead knowing my first IVF cycle was quickly approaching. My work-up had to be complete prior to setting up my cycle calendar. I had a section in my workbook dedicated to all things involved in the work-up and here it is as follows:

- ✔ FSH/LH/E2/AMH – blood test to check ovarian reserve
- ✔ Additional testing TSH/FreeT4/Prolactin/CBC/ Vitamin D
- ✔ APA: Blood test, immune testing
- ✔ Communicable Testing: HIV/HEP B/HEP C/ and RPR. This testing must be current within six months.
- ✔ Chromosome Analysis
- ✔ Cystic Fibrosis, Fragile X, Spinal Muscular Atrophy: Blood test to see if you are at increased risk for giving birth to a child with these genetic disorders.
- ✔ Blood Type and Screen (ABO-RH/antibody) Rubella, Varicella Zoster: Blood test, we need documentation of your blood type and if you are immune to rubella and varicella
- ✔ Baseline Ultrasound/3D: Ultrasound to assess the number of resting follicles, blood flow to the uterus, or presence of any anatomic abnormalities.
- ✔ Office Hysteroscopy: A small fiber optic camera is used to look inside the uterus.
- ✔ Hysterosalpingogram (HSG); Dye is injected to assess if the fallopian tubes are open and that the uterine cavity is normal.
- ✔ Annual Exam/Pap Smear/Mammogram
- ✔ Semen Analysis
- ✔ Anti-sperm antibodies and Culture
- ✔ Sperm Chromatin Structure Assay

This was the work-up calendar I started working on mid-year of 2013, and it continued until completion. By December of 2013, I had started paying close attention to my period from the start date and figured when I was surging or not. I started taking Estrace the day after Christmas and started taking Cetrotide on the 27th. My doctors and nurses started seeing me regularly and sometimes daily to do blood work. Everything was coming together.

January 2014

The New Year had begun and was full of various protocols, appointments, and medications. My IVF cycle calendar had been created. January was the month I had waited months upon months for and worked so hard to achieve. The struggles, and my uphill journey of achieving this part of the process, had finally arrived.

The stimulation phase of IVF was just around the corner; it was the most important step, where the medications I would inject into my own body would generate as many mature eggs as possible.

In the month prior, I was told my stimulation cycle would occur around January 9th and last for at least a ten-day time frame. I had purchased everything I needed for my 2014 IVF cycle package, which included ICSI, CCS, and anesthesia, for a total of $22,435. Once I purchased my meds for my stimulation, I realized the vials and tiny glass tubes of my medications were roughly $1,000's worth daily, multiply it by ten, and that's another $10,000.

Even though this was the part of my journey I had long awaited, I was scared to death. What if I injected the needle wrong? What if I mess up? Oh gosh! I can't mess up; this one medication alone costs $300!

The extreme stress I carried during this time seemed even more intensified. Thankfully, I reviewed the medication protocol repeatedly and read through each medication thoroughly. The CCRM website had a video medication training to follow. I felt ready; I had to be ready.

I had all my medications ready for my stimulation cycle. I was taking Menopur and Follistim to induce ovulation. These medications were responsible for stimulating growth and the maturation of my eggs. I also took Dexamethasone to prevent the excess secretion of male hormones from the adrenal glands. I took the Menopur at 9:35 a.m. every morning starting on the third of January up through the twelfth, and the Follistim at 9:35 p.m. every evening from the third of January up to the twelfth as well.

Blood work was done in the mornings, and I had ultrasounds done every other day towards the end of my stimulation phase. Every day following was to check the size and maturity of each egg on the left and right side of my ovaries.

By January 10th, I began taking Ganirelix to prevent a premature LH surge during my cycle. On the 10th, I also attended a class at CCRM on the CCS testing; CCS stands for Comprehensive Chromosome Screening. This screening is performed on a few cells that will be removed from my day five embryos, also called the blastocyst.

The technology used, polymerase chain reaction, allowed the evaluation of all 23 pairs of human chromosomes on a single cell. Once the cells were tested, my embryos would be stored on ice, until my desired time to do my frozen embryo transfer, also known as FET for those of us educated on the in-vitro fertilization process.

My nurse and I would go over the ultrasound results for each ovary, and we began to keep track of how many mature eggs were forming. These were my findings throughout my stimulation cycle:

Cycle Day 7 (January 6th)
Left ovary – 6, 6, 5, 5, 4.5, 3 = 6 total
Right ovary – 6, 5, 5, 4, 4 = 5 total
Cycle Day 9 (January 8th)
Left ovary – 9, 8, 7.5, 7= 5 eggs
Right ovary – 9, 8, 7 = 4 eggs
Cycle Day 11 (January 10th)
Left ovary – 10, 10, 10, 9, 7, 7 = 7 eggs
Right ovary – 12, 12, 10, 10, 6, 5 = 8 eggs
Cycle Day 13 (January 12th)
Left ovary – 14.2, 13, 12.3, 9.3, 8.2, 7.1, 7.1 = 7 eggs

Right ovary – 14.8, 13.4, 11.1, 8, 8, 7, 6, 5 = 8 eggs

Cycle Day 14 (January 13th)

Left ovary – 14.5, 14.5, 14, 13, 10, 10, 9, 9 = 8 eggs

Right ovary – 15.5, 15, 14, 14, 11, 9.5 = 6 eggs

Cycle Day 15 (January 14th)

Left ovary – 20, 17, 16, 15, 14, 12, 10 = 7 eggs

Right ovary – 19, 17, 17, 17, 11, 10, 9 = 7 eggs

I thought my egg retrieval would be ready for the 14th, but my eggs were not quite mature enough. I was disappointed knowing how much money had already been spent. I had to return to the specialty pharmacy in downtown Denver to purchase two more days' worth, or the equivalent of $2,000 worth of medication. I continued to take the Menopur, Ganirelix, and Follistim on a 9:00 a.m. and 9:00 p.m. protocol.

By the 14th, I had been given permission to attend my IVF physical at 10:30 a.m. that morning. When I was there, I was told my egg retrieval was set for January 16th.

On the morning of the 14th at roughly 7:46 a.m. I remember adding this note into my phone –

"God, you got this, right?
Because I can't do it without you."

The egg retrieval is a surgical procedure, and it was imperative I have a physical prior to it happening. My prep work began early in the morning of January 15th at 1:30 a.m.

with Novarel. This injection was placed in the upper outer quadrant of my buttocks.

Within the next hour, at 2:30 a.m., I injected a trigger shot of Lupron in my stomach. Later that morning, I went in for blood work at 9:30 a.m. to check everything; everything looked great.

Later that afternoon, I injected my final dose of Lupron at 2:30 p.m. I was on a strict protocol leading up to my egg retrieval; I wasn't allowed to eat or drink anything for eight hours prior to my surgical procedure to retract my mature eggs from each of my ovaries.

I arrived at CCRM at 11:30 a.m. and was prepped in my room for my egg retrieval inside their surgical suite. The staff had me change into a gown and surgical cap, and they soon started the IV. I was wheeled into the OR, where I met the doctor who would be performing my egg retrieval, along with my anesthesiologist.

"Adele, start counting back from 100, please. I am going to place this over your mouth," my anesthesiologist calmly said.

"100…99…98…97…" and I slowly drifted off.

I woke up inside the recovery room, completely unaware of everything that had occurred. I spoke softly, as my throat was agitated and sore, "Nurse, please don't forget to retrieve my eggs."

"Adele, we are all done. We already retrieved your eggs. We were able to collect a total of seventeen eggs from both ovaries. Would you like something to drink? You had a reaction to the anesthesia while under the IV sedation, so we ended up having to tube you; this is why your throat is sore. Please take your time and rest."

Wow, I'm done already? Amazing, and 17 eggs, that's incredible!

But this was just the tip of the iceberg; the next 24 to 48 hours were critical, as the eggs would meet the sperm in the lab to see if they would fertilize. The next five days were where all the magic would take place; this was the waiting period to see if the combination of fertilized eggs and sperm would become blastocysts, a.k.a., embryos.

Upon returning from CCRM, I was told to rest my body and stay on bed rest post-op. Within the next 24 hours, I received a call from CCRM; a nurse from the lab called to inform me that 13 of the 17 eggs had taken fertilization through the process of ISCI, (intracytoplasmic sperm injection); the lab tech injects selected sperm directly into the eggs in the lab.

I was told six of the eggs were completely mature and were fertilized. Five of my eggs were still in culture with a possibility of maturing, so they were going to hold onto those five to see if they would reach their potential.

Day 5 Results

Finally, January 22nd had arrived: the day when we would find out whether the eggs fertilized through ISCI would become our blasts – our "embies". The ones we prayed so hard for, for so many years. That afternoon, we received a call from CCRM, and the embryologist told us the following:

- Four blasts were created out of thirteen
- The five that were cultured didn't split and arrested in the fertilization process
- Of the four blasts, the quality of the embies was:
- 5AA
- 3AA
- 3AB
- 3BB

During the IVF process, once your fertilized eggs and sperm become blastocysts, they are graded for their quality. This is how the grading process is broken down:

AA = excellent quality
AB = high quality
BB = Good quality
5 = bigger blast
3 = smaller blast

I was told anything below the BB quality, as well as anything lower than a three, would be more prone to miscarriage, and the embies wouldn't survive the thaw, let alone survive in utero.

On January 28th, we were told two of the four embies we had were 5AA and 3AB quality. While I was completely satisfied knowing I had at least two high-quality embryos, I felt saddened by the fact that all the money that were spent on this cycle and stimulation phase resulted in only two viable embryos.

So many of my friends I met through the support group had at least seven or more embies on ice to use at a later time. I was worried that my chances of conceiving were slim to none with just two embryos. I was concerned about what the outcome would be.

There was so much to be thankful for in knowing we had one successful IVF cycle with two completely healthy embies; yet I knew we weren't out of the woods yet – so many things had to be done and considered.

Since we had opted to do the FET, Frozen Embryo Transfer, with the added benefit of CCS testing and allowing my body to move back to its original state, we were told we could choose any date to do the embryo or embryos' transfer.

We were asked to tell CCRM when my menstrual cycle would begin again. The following day, on January 29th, is when my cycle began. Two days later, I began taking birth control and continued this through the 23rd of February.

Regroup

On February 19, I had a discussion with my doctor about our next steps in deciding when we would like to complete the embryo transfer. We were given the information about our CCS testing and were told that once the embryo transfer was completed and resulted in a positive pregnancy, we would graduate from CCRM after our first trimester. Upon leaving CCRM, we could meet with our geneticist about the embryos we transferred.

The benefit of the CCS testing is also that we would know the gender of our baby prior to our OB appointment, which was wonderful to think about, as most parents do not find out the sex of their growing fetus until later in their pregnancy. I was excited about this news; knowing how difficult this process had been, plus being the organized person I am, with all type A traits, I was thrilled to potentially begin planning my nursery in advance.

There was a blood test I completed during my work-up prior to my stimulation cycle that was set to expire at the end of March of 2014. The test was the communicable diseases: HIV, Hepatitis B, Hepatitis C, and RPR. This test was not covered under my current insurance, and it would be an additional out-of-pocket cost of $500. We decided to forgo paying for another test since its expiration at the six-month mark would occur on March 29, 2014.

We spoke with our doctor and decided to plan our embryo transfer for March 19. After much prayer and thought, we decided to transfer the two embryos we had.

This process had taken a toll on my mental, emotional, and spiritual health throughout the years and months leading up to my egg retrieval. The cost of the work-up, the stimulation cycle, and everything in-between had hit us financially, as well as our loving family members who graciously gave of themselves to get us to this point. I just couldn't imagine going down this road again.

I had a long conversation with God about everything. I told God, "Lord, if you want me to be a mother, you will allow this to happen. I hope and pray this happens for us. My dream is to be a mother. Please listen to the desires of my heart and answer my deepest cry."

Our doctor mentioned my chances of achieving pregnancy with one embryo transferred were a 50/50 chance. However, with transferring both, the chances that one would take were 65%. The thought of transferring only one embryo seemed like a game of chance to me. What if the embryo I chose was the wrong choice? The 50/50 chance didn't sit well with me. This was the driving force that helped us reach our decision to transfer the only two embryos we had. We were also aware of the potential chance of having a multiple birth. I had known this, yet with my history of zero positive pregnancies for several years and all of what took me to this level in needing medical assistance, I didn't mind it. Maybe, just maybe, God would bless me with more than one child.

That day, my doctor started me on Lupron, and I continued this up through March 13. I was also put on baby aspirin to be taken daily up until the transfer, and a Vivelle patch to alternate every other day prior to the transfer. I added additional patches as the weeks led up to the transfer and beyond.

On March 13, I went in for an ultrasound to check my uterine lining, as well as to complete a blood draw. My uterine lining looked excellent, according to the technician. She mentioned there was a triple pattern, and the lining was at 0.96cm, which was above the 0.80cm that CCRM wanted. My estrogen level was 426, which was fantastic because they wanted this number to be above 300. My progesterone was low at 0.1, which was also considered perfect.

On March 14, I started Medrol to be taken once every evening for the next four evenings, as well as Prometrium vaginally at bedtime. The next day, I started Doxycycline, taking it every morning and evening until it was gone. I also began using Endometrin three times daily and progesterone in oil injections every other day intramuscularly. The medicine protocol remained intense even after the stimulation period.

Embryo Transfer Day

The morning of my transfer, I needed to get up extra early to insert an Endometrin capsule and do some prep work for the transfer. Once I finished, I had about an hour to spare before leaving for CCRM. I took out my Bible from my bedside table and opened it to 1 Samuel 1:1-28. I read this story with my sister Aster during our Bible Study. We had read it together, and the words spoke to me. Hannah had been a barren woman for many years; she had turned to God and cried and wept out to Him in her deepest cry to conceive and bear a son. In return, if God would answer her deepest cry, she would give her son back to God.

I read this story again until the words sank in. I got down on my hands and knees and began to pray, "Lord Jesus, I ask that you bless my womb today in my embryo transfer, just as you did years ago with Hannah. Lord Jesus, will you please grant me the gift of being able to carry my own child?" I then folded my hands over my womb and began to cry out, "Jesus, if I am not meant to carry my child here on this earth, I give this child back to you. I give these embryos back into your hands."

The tears turned into sobs, and my heart cried out, as this journey was in its final hour. I knew right then and there that everything would be in God's hands. He had guided me from the Virgin Islands and took me down this incredible path of ups and downs. He built my faith and provided a few miraculous medical reports along the way. This was God's time to shine and for His glory to be magnified.

During my heartfelt and deep prayer, I pulled out my headphones and smartphone, searching for my favorite two songs that were somewhat my lifeline during my IVF cycle: "*Lord, I Need You*" and "*Sovereign*" by Chris Tomlin. I continued to listen to these songs over and over, grasping onto my womb and asking God to bless me with the gift of pregnancy and motherhood.

I knew with God all things were possible. Even though this road led me to many questions and years of unanswered prayers, I felt at peace going into my embryo transfer that morning. It was time to go, so we headed to CCRM to see if our years and years of dreams would be conceivable. This was, of course, the motto for CCRM; I only hoped we could fall into that category.

Upon arrival, I completed a blood draw and continued to drink water to have a partially full bladder prior to the transfer. I chose to be completely relaxed prior to the transfer and had scheduled an acupuncturist who specialized in CCRM embryo transfers to give me pre- and post-acupuncture as my body needed to rest for the next 24 hours.

As my doctor was getting everything ready for the transfer, I was given a Valium to relax, and the embryologist came in to set things up for my doctor. She had a large TV screen magnified multiple times showing our thawed embryos getting ready to be transferred back into my body. They were the most beautiful collection of cells I had ever seen.

I wrote this on the afternoon of the embryo transfer once I had returned home: "It went very well. I'm on strict bed rest, only getting up to use the bathroom. I was given a

Valium and just woke up. Everything took about two hours. I did blood work this morning and my levels for estrogen and progesterone are above where they need to be, which is great. I also did acupuncture before and after the transfer to help relax. I didn't feel a thing. We got to watch him implant the embryos on the ultrasound screen, which was so cool! Akuma was able to take a picture of the embryos before they were inserted. The doctor told me my uterus looked good, and the embryologist said that when they thawed the embryos, they thawed well and were 100%. All the signs look very good! So excited things went well."

Estrogen > 300 = 464
Progesterone > 20 = 22.3

The next nine days post transfer were said to be the hardest nine days of an IVF journey. The waiting period for the next blood draw and then waiting to see if everything that occurred was met with increased hormone levels of both estrogen and progesterone, followed by a call later that afternoon from my nurse with a positive pregnancy test.

On March 20, the day after my transfer, I added this scripture while I was on bed rest: "Satisfy us in the morning with your unfailing love, that we may sing for joy and be glad all our days," quoted from Psalms 90:14 NIV.

Hope was on the rise.

The following week, I spent a lot of time outside enjoying the sunshine and fresh air at my favorite park in my neighborhood. Several times while walking, I saw various twin strollers and laughed at the thought, "What if God blessed my womb twice and both of those embryos took? Wow, how wild would that be?" I laughed at the thought and then questioned, "Well, if I was pregnant, shouldn't I be feeling it?"

It had been a week post transfer, yet I felt no different. The thoughts were unnerving, and I constantly played Russian roulette in my mind with the various things I was feeling emotionally, spiritually and physically.

March 28, 2014

The day of my blood draw arrived. I reached CCRM early that morning at 7:30 a.m. to get first dibs at getting poked and left, full of nerves and anxiety. I knew I would be receiving a call sometime in the afternoon from my nurse with my results.

I was taken aback when I received a call from the nurse line at 10:50 a.m. I panicked because I thought it was too early to hear from my nurse.

"Good morning, is this Adele? Good morning, Adele, this is Erin from CCRM. I wanted to congratulate you on achieving a positive pregnancy. As a matter of fact, you are **very** pregnant. We want your first HCG test to be above 150 for a viable pregnancy; your first score is 477. We will have you come back in two days' time to complete the next blood draw. We would like to see this number double again. See you then, and once again, congratulations to you and Akuma!"

Nothing could have prepared me for this moment; I couldn't believe I was pregnant. My dream had come true. I had achieved everything I worked so hard to achieve – that one positive pregnancy test to show off to all my family and friends.

After I spoke with Erin, I had asked her to call back and leave a voicemail of everything she had told me on my phone, so I could listen to the results she shared with me repeatedly. I was so overjoyed, it was an incredible accomplishment after years of prayers, tears, and hard work. As soon as Erin left her message, I called my two girlfriends I had met through CCRM's fertility support group to share the news with them. We cried on the phone together with gratitude in our hearts. After I spoke with them, I spoke with my friend Winston about surprising Akuma at work with the news.

On my way down to see him, I dropped by a bookstore to purchase a pregnancy journal and then a gift shop and bought a small pair of shoes as a way to share the news with him.

Akuma comes from an Afro-Caribbean background, with some of his roots in Jamaica. I wanted to share the news of the pregnancy with something that would remind him of his roots.

During my last IUI with CCRM in May of 2013, which had failed, I bought these M&M's in the colors of Jamaica that read the words – "Baby Rasta, Dis Pikny, One Love and Jah Bless." In Jamaican, the word "pikny" means child.

It gave me great joy to give him this message in a bottle with all the colorful green, yellow, and black M&M's. I had stored this same glass bottle in my closet since 2013 and prayed for the day I would be able to give it to him. Today was the day, and I couldn't have been more thrilled.

I arrived in downtown Denver and met Winston in the hotel lobby to share the news. He greeted me with the biggest smile on his face. We spoke briefly about how to surprise Akuma and put the plan into action. Winston brought me up to the club level and hid me in the kitchen to surprise him. Winston went and pulled him aside to bring him to me, and Akuma said, "Wow, what are you doing here?"

I replied," I have a gift for you."

"Oh, okay, but what are you doing here?" he curiously responded.

"Open the gift and look inside, Akuma," I said excitedly.

Akuma pulled out the message bottle, quickly glanced over the M&Ms, thumbed through the bag, and pulled out the baby shoes. He still looked very puzzled, and I finally yelled out, "Akuma, we're pregnant! It worked! Our first IVF cycle worked!" I cried happy tears and everyone in the room was full of enthusiasm. Akuma seemed so surprised. We took a few pictures, and then I headed out to the grocery store to pick up a pregnancy test. I knew this time…this time, I would see the results I prayed so many years for.

Now it was time to share the news with my family and all my friends who had prayed for years along with me for this very moment.

This moment had finally arrived. I was so euphoric.

March 30, 2014 (Week 5) Journal Notes

Today, I returned to CCRM to receive my second HCG blood draw. My nurse Erin told me that if I had a viable pregnancy, my numbers would double. The number from my first draw was 477, and now it is 1303. The pregnancy is viable, and the embryo or embryos are latching onto my uterine wall, and this pregnancy is thriving.

I was told to return on April 14th for my first vaginal ultrasound. It was a procedure to see if we could find out what we were having. I was hoping to have dreams at bedtime to figure out what was growing inside me to give myself some kind of intuition, yet I never had any dreams about being pregnant.

Upon returning from my second blood draw, I pulled out my pregnancy journal and answered this question:

Stop for a moment and meditate on the wonder of a God who can create a heart. If He can coordinate the timing of microscopic cells to begin beating, why do we doubt His timing in any area of our lives? If He can cause a single cell to jolt awake, how much more is He capable of bringing something out of nothing in our lives? In what areas do you need to trust Him more? Affirm that He is worthy of your trust.

...after going through the four years and eight months of infertility and IVF and putting my heart out there in the *Breaking Free* Beth Moore study – I trust God completely.

April 14, 2014 (Week 7) Journal Notes

Akuma and I arrived at CCRM for my first vaginal ultrasound. We went back into the room and I got prepped for the appointment. The ultrasound technician told me she would be checking my uterine lining and making sure nothing was going on with my ovaries.

She asked me to lie back, get comfortable, and then she took the probe and inserted it to begin looking around. At first glance, the probe focused on my uterus, and it displayed two heartbeats on the screen.

The nurse looked up at the screen and said, "Adele, you are pregnant with twins!"

I looked at Akuma and my jaw dropped. I couldn't believe what I was hearing.

Then, the tech said, "Okay, let me go around and look at the lining and ovaries.... oh wait, hold on...oh my gosh, Adele...one embryo has split; you are actually pregnant with TRIPLETS!"

I froze. I stared at the screen. I looked at Akuma. I couldn't even speak. What in the world?

I sat there and told the tech, “Whoa, can you please print all of those off for me?” Oh my gosh. Triplets? Wait till everyone I know finds out. Ha!

As I was getting ready to leave the ultrasound suite, the hallway was lined with doctors and nurses, and everyone was clapping as we walked down the hall to get my blood work done. It was surreal. This was real, though, and it was truly incredible.

We left CCRM and headed over to Babies “R” Us to set up our registry. I wanted to get the ball rolling and get everything set up. I knew we were going to need to get as much help from my community and family.

Triplets.... Never in my life did I ever imagine this. Never. Wow. We were triply blessed. We definitely received more than we prayed for.

When we were setting up our registry, the store manager Faith was extremely helpful to us. She walked around the store with us and told us about each product and what we would need, as well as the best options for bottles, car seats, and pretty much anything you could possibly think of, and at times triple of everything. The list grew longer and longer as we scanned various items throughout the store.

Before leaving the store, I found three rubber duckies of various sizes and decided that this would be how we would share the big, big news with my family. I bought a random gift bag and threw in the duckies that I labeled Baby A, Baby B, and Baby C. This all made sense to Akuma and me. From now on, every time I had an ultrasound with my tech at CCRM, the babies would be named this.

We set out to surprise my mom and my good friend Lucy, who helped with some of my first injections during my stimulation phase that evening.

Akuma and I set the bag on the table, and we told my mom and Lucy to look in the bag.

My mom asked, "Do you know what you are having?"

"Mom, we don't know the sex, but we do know what we are having," I smiled and told her.

"Oh, I thought you knew!" she gasped.

They pulled the bag closer to them and began sifting through it. They put their hands in the bag and began looking around towards the bottom of the bag.

They both looked at each other and said, "WHAT? Wait... what? Are you kidding me? Wait... what? No way!" Lots of nervous laughter ensued, and their jaws dropped, "Are you kidding me? What? Oh my gosh, Adele, really? There are one, two, three babies!"

We told them we were in shock just as much as they were. The news of having triplets was unbelievable. I continued to share the delightful news with my other close friends. This was everything I waited years to share.

My sweet friend Lucy told me the meaning of three means "protection of God, strength and wisdom".

Marie told me, "I was just thinking about it and just think it is so cool how faithful God is proving to be in your life. At one point, you felt cursed because of not being able to conceive, and he totally showed up here to show you he is present and showering you with the most amazing blessing possible. How cool. God is so, so faithful and hears our cries. Thank you for reminding me how amazing our God is and how much he loves me. What a testimony you have!"

April 25, 2014 (Week 8) Journal Notes

After finding out about my triplet pregnancy, I wanted to make sure I could carry all three in my growing womb. I met with my doctor again, and he suggested meeting with a specialist in multiple pregnancies and births who is well known all over Colorado for his expertise in this area, so I made an appointment to meet with him.

Akuma and I drove to his office at Presbyterian St. Luke's Medical building. We spoke about my triplet pregnancy, looked at my growing babies through ultrasound, and he explained to me the options of carrying all three babies. He mentioned the possibility of eliminating the multiple conception, and he suggested the elimination of the twins growing inside me. Everything was spoken so quickly, and it never dawned on me exactly as he was saying – elimination of the twins.

He had me schedule the appointment, as it was a hard procedure to schedule and get in. The appointment for the elimination was set for May 23rd.

After the whirlwind of the appointment, the more I grasped what he was saying, I did a quick turnaround. I canceled the appointment an hour after making it, as I knew I could never abort what God gave me.

The thought of ever killing the very lives I prayed years for was not an option or a choice. I had a very intimate conversation with God and I told him, "Lord, if you want me to carry triplets to full term, you Lord, will make this happen. If you want me to become a triplet mama, then this is what I was meant to do – and if not, you will take the life from me on your terms in my womb or otherwise, but Lord, I will not make this decision. I didn't come this far in my faith and prayer life to achieve my dreams of this amazing triplet pregnancy to eliminate it."

The specialist supported my decision and told me my multiple pregnancy would be taken care of in the best hands and doctors going forward.

As soon as I graduated from CCRM with my first trimester, I would then attend the medical practice that specialized in high risk pregnancies and multiple births for the remainder of my pregnancy and birth of my children.

Pregnancy Journal Entries

1st Trimester symptoms

March 28, 2014 – Breast tenderness, fatigue, frequent urination

April 2014 - Backache, breast tenderness, constipation, diarrhea, fatigue, frequent urination, heartburn, leg cramps, moodiness, nausea, vomiting
May 2014 – Backache, bloating, breast tenderness, constipation, fatigue, frequent urination, headaches, heartburn, vomiting, hemorrhoids, nausea, vaginal discharge

May 7, 2014 (Week 10)
First time hearing all three heartbeats
Baby A – 180
Baby B – 186
Baby C – 174
I cried when I heard each heartbeat. It was music to my ears and just another reminder of God's promises to me.

May 12, 2014 (Week 11)
I'm looking forward to holding each of my children in my arms and feeding them, rocking them to sleep, tucking them in at night, praying with them, singing to them, and playing with them.

May 19, 2014 (Week 12)
Today is the final day for all my IVF meds! I will soon graduate from CCRM and begin attending my multiple birth/high-risk OB doctor.

May 20, 2014

Today my geneticist told me what we are having. I found out we are having identical twin boys and a girl. Oh my goodness, the best of everything in one!

I was so elated to relay the news to Akuma and the rest of the family once I returned home from my final consultation with my doctor. During the consultation, my geneticist told me what we were having. I had gone to a gift shop and purchased a variety of pink and blue bubble gum cigars and had them wrapped in ribbon that read, "Baby Girl and Baby Boy". I wrapped two of the baby boys together with one pink and shared the news over dinner that day with Akuma. He was thrilled.

I shared the information with my mom as I took her to the airport for a flight departure the following morning. I handed her a small bag with the bubble gum cigars, and as she opened it she squealed with excitement.

As fun as it was to give everyone the bubble gum cigars, it was just as joyful for me too. I couldn't believe God had blessed my womb three times over and was giving me the gift of raising identical twin boys and a girl. Wow, what an incredible moment and gift of growing three babies in my womb.

May 25, 2014 (Week 13)

Last blood work at CCRM. I graduated

Estrogen = 6,768

Progesterone = 76

May 29, 2014

My second OB appointment today – I was told I could eat chocolate (yay!) dark chocolate, have one cup of coffee a day, continue taking the baby aspirin, and I could use a swimming pool to relax. All of the babies are healthy, and their heartbeats are strong. The babies are very active!

God, I thank you every day for my sweet loves. Thank you for letting me experience being pregnant and seeing my loves on the ultrasound screen.

I pray for those who still struggle with the unknown. May you comfort them and remind them they are cared for and loved.

On June 1st, on my way to church, I bought myself my first tall latte in over a year's time. I couldn't wait for my first sip of creamy, delicious hot caffeine. I waited upon arrival to drink it and enjoy every morsel.

Awe, it was so good going down…not so great coming right back up. Haha! That short moment of deliciousness was delayed for the rest of my pregnancy.

Second Trimester Journal Entries

2nd Trimester Symptoms

June 2014 – Insomnia

July 2014 – Backaches, breast tenderness, fatigue, frequent urination, heartburn, insomnia, leg cramps, nausea, swollen feet, vaginal discharge, wrist pain, hand numbness

August 2014 – Acne and skin problems, allergies, crying spells, frequent urination, hip pain, insomnia, sore knees, swollen feet, urine leakage, vaginal discharge

June 4, 2014 (Week 14)
I have continued daily to lay hands on my belly to pray for my little ones in their weekly development and growth. I am so thankful the babies are all healthy and survived the first trimester. I was so nervous that with three, some wouldn't make it, but they all did. I love getting to see their development as they continue to grow. I look forward to the ultrasounds every time.

June 15, 2014 (Week 15)
Last night was the first night I didn't go to bed nauseous. I know through this pregnancy He is glorified. My children have a God who is all-powerful and all-knowing. The names have been chosen and I pray for them by name.

Even before my transfer, I had always laid my hands on my womb, praying for the embies to stick and to grow inside me. I had made it an act of love and a prayerful place of praise, not knowing one day God would reward me with what I know now. I was going to become a mom, a phenomenal mom to triplets. I knew the importance of prayer, and it meant so much to me to do this sacred act; there was so much purpose in my prayers.

June 17, 2014
All the babies' heartbeats are between 150 – 160 beats per minute. They look healthy, and all of their stomachs and bladders are working.

Lord, please allow me to trust my husband fully in order to respect him as the head of our household. Let me leave the mistrust and how he's failed me – in the past. Provide me with ways to trust him more.

June 24, 2014 (Week 16)
I love you beyond measure. I will make sacrifices here and there to support you throughout your life. God, give me the provision to plan for my babies in advance to supply their needs. My pregnancy is already bringing family members out of the darkness and into the light. We are so excited to see what God is doing in the midst and are so gracious and thankful.

I met a triplet mom group through Facebook and met these triplet mamas for dinner at a local Mexican restaurant. I was assigned a mentor from here on, till through my delivery of the triplets.

I was advised by many of the moms to begin having my baby showers and to have them done prior to the 3rd trimester. I listened to many tragic stories of moms not being able to bring all their babies' home from the hospital or NICU due to complications in- utero or extremely premature births. I also listened to moms sharing how they were on hospital bed rest for months leading up to their birth and how many of their babies had complications upon delivery.

It made me panic a bit, so I knew each week from here on – was a huge accomplishment; week by week was rewarded and seen as a blessing. I had many baby showers planned and in the works leading up to the 3rd trimester.

June 27, 2014 (Week 17)

Praying all this week for your bones to harden and that you are getting the calcium you need. I also pray that your heart will remain soft so that God can use you in mighty ways.

July 9, 2014 (Week 19)

I felt movement inside for the first time today. I was in my water aerobics class working out when I felt this jolt and heaviness on the lower left side of my belly. It made me stop in my tracks – I tried to feel them with my hands, but it didn't happen.

July 14, 2014

Anatomy scan went well today. All babies are super healthy and above schedule.

July 18, 2014 (Week 20)

Dear Loves,

Only God knows how I yearned for you for years. He is a miracle worker and loves to bless his people. May each of you fall in love with Him over and over and never lose sight of his love and wisdom.

July 27, 2014 (Week 21)
Baby Shower #1 with my church family

July 28, 2014
Ultrasound and cervix check - cervix looks great and fluid looks great with all babies.

Father, please show me where pride stands in the way of developing a more intimate relationship with my husband. Teach me to be more humble and understanding.

July 29, 2014
7:53 P.M. I felt baby C (Scarlett) move for the first time with my hand on my belly.

Lord, please guide us as the months get closer to when we will hold and care for our children. Make us a strong couple that raises our children together; that we will put our wants on the back burner and put their needs first.

July 30, 2014 (Week 22)
I received three high chairs from my dad today. The first gift in eleven years. The first time he made an effort in eleven years. I'm speechless.

August 2, 2014
Baby Shower #2 at our neighbor's house with all of my closest friends.

I would love to see my husband read his Bible more or do a devotion, rather than spend so much time on his phone. I would love to grow closer to him by doing and being committed to study the Bible together.

I desire to see less technology in our marriage, especially cell phones and TV. I feel like it is disconnecting us from each other – to the point that if we went out on an outing, we wouldn't have much to talk about. I am going to pray that this will change.

August 11, 2014 (Week 23)
Babies are healthy and growing on schedule – the twins weigh 1.7 pounds/ounces, while my daughter weighs 1.5 pounds/ounces

August 13, 2014 (Week 24)
From the very beginning of my pregnancy, I knew that these souls were to be glorified by God. I feel completely covered in His garment in this pregnancy. I thank God every day for entrusting these souls to me. Scarlett, Kingston, and Reece, may you all come to know the one who brought you into this world. I was the "Lucky vessel" God used. May you know how much He loves you and wants to know you and bless you.

August 16, 2014
Baby Shower #3 at my mom's house with close friends and family

I was so disappointed in Akuma's behavior once he came home from work to celebrate with his friends about our upcoming birth of the triplets. I felt completely disrespected in front of his friends and my mom. I had to leave and went to our room and remained behind closed doors till the morning. I cannot believe how rude he was. I waited patiently for him to arrive, so we could all share a meal together. He offered everyone a drink, except me, and basically told me to go get my own glass of water. I cannot believe his ill treatment towards me. Thankfully, his friends pulled him aside and gave it to him and set him straight. I will not tolerate this behavior.

August 20, 2014 (Week 25)
First reunion with my dad and his wife in eleven years, dinner out on the town, and they meet Akuma for the first time.

I have already set up the nursery and have most of the bottles I need for each baby. I've also signed up to take a breastfeeding class in order to prepare feeding multiples. I'm looking to sign up for a childbirth prep/Getting to know your newborn class soon.

August 26, 2014
Akuma had his interview this morning to become a citizen of the United States. He passed 100%. I am so proud of him.

August 27, 2014 (Week 26)
Baby Shower #4 with mom's friends at her work

September 5, 2014 (Week 27)
Three-hour glucose test day

Third Trimester Journal Entries

3rd Trimester Symptoms
September 2014 – Anxiety, backache, constipation, dry mouth while sleeping, fatigue, frequent urination, gas, heartburn, hip pain, insomnia, itching all over, leg cramps
October 2014 – Anxiety, backache, congestion, crampy, dizzy, dry mouth while sleeping, fatigue, frequent urination, gas, heartburn, hip pain, insomnia, itching all over, leg cramps, nausea, panic attacks, pelvic pressure, sore knees, swollen feet, urine leakage

September 10, 2014 (Week 28)
I passed the three-hour glucose test with flying colors! Praise God!

Some of the highlights of my pregnancy include **no complications** – even though I am considered high risk.

No signs of TTTS – Twin-to-twin transfusion syndrome –, which is a rare pregnancy condition affecting identical twins or other multiples. TTTS occurs in pregnancies where twins share the same placenta and a network of blood vessels that supply oxygen and nutrients essential for development in the womb. I am not anemic, nor do I have gestational diabetes. The babies are all active, healthy, and their fluid levels and weights are normal. My cervix is above 2.5 and I'm not on bed rest. Whoo-Hoo, God gets the glory for this!

September 11, 2014
Reece weighs 2.9 pounds
Kingston weighs 2.8 pounds
Scarlett 2.15 pounds
All are healthy, and fluid looks good.

September 19, 2014
Akuma gets his U.S. citizenship!

September 24, 2014 (Week 30)
I loved you before you were conceived. I prayed for you, wishing one day I would be your mother. I cried over you with joy. I prayed over you every day during pregnancy. I have dreamt about meeting you and holding you in my arms. You are so loved.

September 26, 2014

I planned my own impromptu maternity shoot. We drove up to Guanella Pass to take pictures of my pregnant belly. The aspen trees were absolutely stunning.

September 29, 2014

I am so thankful for this pregnancy and so thankful that God has allowed me to become a mother, not just to one baby, but three at once. These babies are my beautiful gifts.

October 8, 2014 (Week 32)

Lord, as this due date approaches, please discipline me enough to have quiet times with you and to depend on you to provide for our family and our basic needs.

Psalms 29:11 NIV "The Lord will give strength to his people; the Lord will bless his people with peace."

I've been through a lot of difficulties in my life, but God has always strengthened me and given me peace about my circumstances.

October 9, 2014

Kingston weighs 3.11 pounds
Reece weighs 4 pounds
Scarlett weighs 4.5 pounds

October 10, 2014

I have seen evidence of doing the will of the Father after doing the Breaking Free study by Beth Moore. I learned I have to trust God with everything in my life, that I cannot do it alone. I also learned how much he loves me.

I have my hospital bag packed for my husband, my babies, and me, ready to go. I have some numbers on hand as well.

October 14, 2014 (Week 33)

Lately, I've been feeling at my worst in the afternoon, and I tend to take naps then. I'm also feeling the weight of the babies and it wears me out.

I pray each of your brains are fully developed, and your weights are that of a full-term baby. May you all make it to our desired due date.

October 17, 2014

May you continue to grow, and may your weights be considered full term when you are born. As each of you enter this world, may you grow in wisdom, stature, and favor in the eyes of God. May others know you are blessed.

October 21, 2014 (Week 34)

I was put on bed rest this afternoon. I have started to have symptoms of preeclampsia – high blood pressure, swelling of my feet, excessive weight gain in just two weeks, and protein was found in my urine. I was told to monitor my blood pressure over the next week and if it rises above 150/90, I would need to call in and potentially be put on hospital bed rest.

October 22, 2014

I know that taking care of three little newborns will be a challenge in itself on top of all other tasks at hand, so I know I'll need to depend on others and get to know Christ all the more as this new journey begins.

Reece, Kingston and Scarlett – may all of your ambitions be holy and bring glory to God. May you speak kindly, be grateful, and be good stewards in your home, school and community.

October 23, 2014

I know that everyone is different, but for the most part, I've gotten great responses about my pregnant body. I know that God doesn't see the stretch marks or weight gain – he sees no flaw in me.

Kingston, Reece and Scarlett – may you know that God's approval is all you need. He hand-knit you together in my womb, and his workmanship is marvelous. The outside of your body will always change, but what truly matters is what lies in your heart.

October 24, 2014

This evening, I checked my blood pressure, and it was 161/100. It was extremely high. I went ahead and called the after-hours line at my OB office, and they told me to have Akuma drive me to the hospital and get checked in to the Labor and Delivery floor.

I was so annoyed by all of this. At this point, the pregnancy hormones came into view; I thought for sure if I was to eat a salad, my blood pressure would have dropped. I was so wrong.

We packed our hospital bags and headed for the hospital downtown. I cried all the way there. The only thing I could think of was having my babies before November. I hated Halloween so much and I didn't want to have costume parties for their birthday. Once again, the hormones came into play.

We had to meet at the emergency department, so we could enter the hospital to get checked in after hours, plus I couldn't walk on my own and needed to have wheelchair assistance.

I arrived at the L&D floor, and all the night nurses were so excited for me, "Wow, you are having triplets! Congratulations!"

All I did was cry and say, "They are gonna be October babies, aren't they?"

Once the nursing staff set up the baby monitors for Baby A, Baby B, and Baby C it was nearly 10 p.m. I was told I could have a few more sips of water, but past midnight nothing, just in case, I was to deliver the following day.

I couldn't believe it. Deliver? I was not ready for that. I was leaning more towards the hospital bed rest my favorite nurse practitioner was warming me up to. That definitely sounded way more appealing, at least for the next eight days as it was my goal to get to November 1st. Ha! The odds were against me, but I was hopeful to at least get through a few more days if not those eight days. I definitely did not want to have Halloween babies.

Over the month of October, I really struggled with quite a few pregnancy symptoms: anxiety, backaches, congestion, feeling crampy, dizzy, having a dry mouth while sleeping, fatigue, frequent urination, gas, heartburn, hip pains, insomnia, itching all over, leg cramps, nausea, panic attacks, pelvic pressure, sore knees, swollen feet due to the preeclampsia, and urine leakage. The symptoms that really took a toll on me started from week 32 up through week 34 were the insomnia and panic attacks. The panic attacks stemmed from all the weight of carrying the triplets, and I began to feel claustrophobic in my own skin. At nighttime, I often slept in the living room with the light on, reclined in my chair.

Once the baby monitors were set, I resumed my routine of having the light on, but this time I was reclining on my hospital bed on the Labor and Delivery floor. I was thankful I remembered to pack my cell phone and my earphones so I could listen to my favorite worship song on my pregnancy playlist – "*Every Praise*" by Hezekiah Walker. I stayed up past midnight listening to this song until I was able to fall asleep.

Early in the morning, the nursing staff took my vitals, checked the baby monitors, and reviewed some regulatory protocols from the medical staff.

Later that morning, I was told the on-call doctor from my OB office would be coming in to look at my labs and speak with me about my potential delivery.

Around 10:00 a.m., Dr. Patrick came into my hospital room with his staff.

"Good morning, Mr. Campbell and Mrs. Charles, we have looked at your charts and your lab work, and we see you have had a wonderful pregnancy so far. We have been monitoring your progress and are paying close attention to the preeclampsia you have developed over the course of the past few weeks. We feel knowing the babies are healthy and you are mostly healthy, that we don't want to take any chances of the preeclampsia getting more severe and we, *as he looks down at his watch,* we would like to, let's see here, how about we set up delivery to occur in 45 minutes?"

WAIT.... WHAAATTTT! Forty-five minutes till delivery? I was in no way ready to hear what came out of Dr. Patrick's mouth. Deliver now? Before November? I was going to have October babies. Oh no...

I quickly called my mom and gave her the latest update since we notified her of the late evening drive to the ED to be admitted to the hospital just hours before. She was so excited and told us she was already in her car and was on her way to the hospital to visit us. She was only minutes away when we made the call.

After I got off the phone, the preparations for the delivery were being made on the L&D floor. So many doctors, nurses, and medical personnel were making way for the delivery. I met with my anesthesiologist, Dr. Anderson, to get me prepped for the cesarean delivery.

Once the spinal block was set up, I was laid upon the steel operating table and looked around the room to notice there were four nurses assigned with one doctor to each neonatal isolette, a team of five for each baby born. There must have been around 20-30 medical professionals to help in the OR the day of the delivery.

October 25, 2014

Scarlett, Kingston's and Reece's birthday.

"Adele, how are you feeling after the spinal block?" asked Dr. Anderson.

"I know you mentioned that I wouldn't feel anything from the waist down, and I can't move my legs or my toes. I'm reminding myself this is normal, so I am working on not panicking about it. I feel comfortable though," I responded.

"Yes, it's a different feeling to experience, but this is what we need to happen as we get ready for the delivery. We have the oxygen set up, the blood pressure monitor set up, and in just a few minutes, I will set up your IV fluid. As you are lying here on the table, your arms will stretch out like a cross, and on your left arm, I will insert the needle to get your IV set up and get you started on IV fluids. If you need anything during your delivery, I will be sitting next to you on your left for the entire delivery. Your husband will be able to sit on the right side of you. If you need anything, or if you have any questions, please let me know. I am here to help you throughout everything." Dr. Anderson stated.

The Birth of the Triplets

I anxiously awaited the arrival of this beautiful day. So many trials, so many years were delayed conceiving, and months of learning how to take care of what God blessed my womb with while watching diligently week by week as they each developed in that secret place.

Dr. Patrick told me everything as it occurred in real time. I knew when he cut into the first layer of my skin, proceeding through to the seventh layer, to pull out Baby A - my precious Reece.

Dr. Patrick announced to the room, "Here is baby A."

I waited for a moment and suddenly heard a loud scream. Tears welled up in my eyes, and I knew Reece was here.

Reece was handed to a nurse who quickly walked around the blue surgery dressing to show me baby A. I got a quick glance at him before he was taken to his team with his isolette ready for his arrival. He was born in a vertex position at 10:42 a.m. and had an APGAR score of 9 out of 9.

Right around this time, I started to feel different. My happiness about the birth and the triplet delivery came with intense waves of nausea. I leaned over to Dr. Anderson and quietly said, "Dr. Anderson, I feel like I'm going to throw up."

A quick thought went through my mind – I had stopped eating around 8 p.m. the night before and only had a few sips of water before midnight – what could I possibly throw up at this time?

"Okay, Adele I have an emesis bag to the left of you if you need to vomit; I am holding it here for you," Dr. Anderson advised.

I leaned to the left and vomited once, twice and a third time. It had to have been bile because my stomach was empty. I proceeded to feel dizzy and disoriented. It felt as if the room was spinning around me.

About a minute later Baby B – my sweet son Kingston was born.

"Here is baby B," Dr. Patrick happily stated.

Once again, a loud scream was heard, and another nurse wrapped Kingston up in swaddling clothes and walked around the curtain to show me baby B. He was then taken to his team at the awaited isolette, and he was taken care of. Kingston was born breech with an APGAR score of 8 out of 9.

Everything became chaotic quickly. I looked at Dr. Anderson again and softly said, "I don't feel well at all, something doesn't feel right. I'm starting to feel dizzy and cold."

At last, Dr. Patrick held up baby C and announced, "Here is baby C."

Scarlett came out and announced her arrival to the world with an immense shout as well. My darling Scarlett was born Frank breech and had an APGAR score of 8 out of 9. A nurse had swaddled Scarlett and brought her to me. She was beautiful.

I leaned over to see her and felt confused, weak, and out of breath. I glanced up at the wall and read the blood pressure screen. My pressure was 80 over 53. I was on the cusp of hypotension.

Unknown to me, Akuma was asked to leave the OR and wait outside. A nurse walked out one of the doors of the OR to meet my mom in the hallway.

"Congratulations, you have three very healthy triplets. We usually never see triplets come out this healthy with a premature birth," the nurse firmly stated.

"That's because these three were prayed over from conception to this delivery," my mom happily responded.

At this time, the three isolettes were whisked away to the highest-level NICU at Rocky Mountain Hospital for Children, which was connected to Presbyterian St. Luke's where the surgery took place.

In the meantime, I rolled my head sloppily to the left to look at Dr. Anderson and noticed the medical staff was changing the IV fluids from saline over to blood.

One male nurse had the tubing in his hands with a small area where the tubing looked like a plastic lime shape in the middle. I realized he was squeezing the lime-shaped tubing cord as fast as he could, as if he was squeezing each heartbeat back into my chest. I realized things had taken a turn for the worse.

Little did I know as I lay there, my mom was pacing back and forth in the hallway outside of the OR praying for the triplets and me.

As she was pacing, several medical professionals ran past her with three coolers of packed red blood cells and entered the OR where I lay.

As I lay fighting for my life, the room seemed full of life and movement, yet I lay in waiting for my soul to leave my body. I knew I was dying. My breath seemed to be short, my heartbeat raced, my body struggled to deliver oxygen and nutrients to tissues in my body which led me to feel incredibly weak and fatigued. Because of the reduced blood flow to my brain, I was severely confused; due to the low blood pressure and the extreme blood loss, I was very lightheaded and dizzy. My heart was working overtime to compensate for the blood loss, and my pulse became weak and thready.

A hallmark symptom of extreme blood loss is where blood pressure drops significantly, and that very thing occurred once all the triplets were successfully delivered.

The coldness I felt was because my body was diverting blood from my extremities to my vital organs, while it was working hard to postpone cardiac arrest, possible unconsciousness leading to a coma, and potentially my death.

Dr. Patrick and his team worked tirelessly for an extended time to control the extreme blood loss and stop the bleeding. It was a race against time for the doctors and nursing staff to use massive transfusion protocols of four packed red blood cell transfusions to administer the PRBC's by rapid infusion equipment to move the blood rapidly back to my body. His team replaced liters of my blood within minutes to save my life.

Dr. Patrick departed the OR and met my mom and Akuma in the hallway.

"Adele has lost a lot of blood. If we cannot get the bleeding under control, we will have to do a complete hysterectomy. For now, she is stable enough to go to the recovery room post-op where we will keep a close eye on her for bleeding. Akuma, you are now welcome to come back to the OR to be with your wife."

Due to being quite disoriented, I didn't realize Akuma had left, nor did I realize he was sitting right next to me.

"Del, do you want me to go be with the babies or would you like me to stay here with you?" Akuma asked.

"Please stay here with me. I need you here," I calmly responded.

I asked the nursing staff if I could see the triplets' placentas and umbilical cords as I lay there on the OR table, as they were working on suturing me up to prepare me to move to the recovery room.

"We never get this request, but sure, let me go get it for you, Adele," replied one of the OR nurses.

She brought over this huge white bucket. I could only lean a bit to the right to glance down into the bucket. It was filled almost to the rim with the placentas, cord blood, my blood, and the white umbilical cords. The bucket was filled to the rim with a red and white substance.

I looked at all of it and told the nurse, "This is everything that provided my babies with life. It's so amazing to see and who knew the umbilical cords were white. How stupendous is that!"

The nurses and I shared a laugh and then it was time for me to get ready to move to the recovery room. Akuma was asked once again to leave the OR and wait in the hallway for further instructions.

The Departure from the OR

Dr. Patrick and his medical team were finishing up on the last few steps before I was ready to be moved to the hospital gurney into the recovery room. The blue curtain was lowered, and to my shock and quick realization, I saw with my own eyes how dangerously close I came to my demise. My eyes met Dr. Patrick's blue surgical gown, and from about his waist up, I saw splatters of my blood upon his chest. Dried splatters peppered the surface of his gown in angry bursts, some sharp-edged and spiky, others smeared by hands. I then glanced over to other medical staff and noticed the same splatter effect on two other surgical assistants.

In front of my feet, in the near distance from the OR table, was a metal medical stand that stood about seven feet from the ground, holding a blue cloth with pockets filled in every nook and cranny of bloodied gauze. Crumbled up, stained in scarlet and lay discarded like battlefield remnants, while other towels and sheets lay oozing their contents onto the surgical floor.

"Okay, Ms. Charles, we are getting ready to move you from the OR table to the gurney to wheel you into the recovery room," mentioned the OR staff, "on the count of three, let's move her...one...two...three..."

Once I was moved over, I glanced over in horror at what I had just left. The OR table had blood dripping from what looked like a white sheet. The white sheet was drenched in blood and looked like a deflated flag, heavy and limp, sagging under the weight of its own sorrow. The drippings plunged into the vast bloodied puddles that surrounded the OR table. It pooled in irregular shapes, like liquid shadows stretching across the floor. The puddles shimmered faintly under the OR light, catching reflections of table legs and scattered objects above. Thin rivulets snaked outward from the main pools, tracing the surgical room floor and into the cracks of its tiled floor. The blood's surface trembled slightly, disturbed by the consistent drip from the table's edge, sending gentle ripples outward like whispers spreading through silence.

The OR table was a chaotic canvas of red blood, as if a storm of color had exploded and settled in thick, uneven layers as the blood began to clot. The air was sharp with the tang of blood; the table and room looked like a horrific crime scene – raw, reckless and surreal.

At last, I was wheeled towards the exit of the OR where I met Akuma and my mom outside.

"Can you please take my phone with you, Akuma, to take some pictures of the babies? I want to see what they look like. Here, please take my phone with you and bring it back," I asked with great care.

I was wheeled into a room right next to the OR and met a nurse who would oversee my care. She let me know I would be there for roughly two hours post-op to make sure the bleeding would stay under control, and it would give me a chance to rest after the whole ordeal.

She continued to check my vitals, and Dr. Patrick would come and go often to press down on my abdomen to see whether the bleeding would gush out or if it was starting to subside. I had no feeling still in the lower half of my body and couldn't grasp what was going on when he came back and pressed down on my abdomen. Since my phone was with Akuma, I had no way to know what was going on in the NICU or what time it was.

The recovery room was cold and still, wrapped in the sterile silence that felt heavier than the weight in my body of all the trauma that occurred in the OR earlier. The walls, drained of color, loomed blank and expressionless – bland, tan, something in between – indistinguishable from the ceiling, like the inside of a box meant to contain pain. I lay motionless, sifting through the silence of the space, which churned with fear, shock, and the love of what I birthed out of my womb in equal measure.

Machines beeped steadily nearby, indifferent to the storm that had passed through me. Eyes fixed to the wall, I tried to find a shape in the bland expanse, something to hold onto – but there was nothing. Just stillness, antiseptic air, and the echo of what had just happened.

Several hours passed, and I realized I was there past the time of two hours, which Dr. Patrick originally said. I lay motionless in that colorless room in solitude for over four hours with only visits from Dr. Patrick and the nurse who took care of me.

Finally, I was given the okay to move out of recovery to a private hospital room near the OR to continue my recovery from the C-section. The private room was a quiet sanctuary, bathed in soft natural light that filtered through the sheer white curtains, casting a gentle glow across the space. The walls were painted warm, calming, tones-muted sage and misty blue – that brought a sense of peace and comfort.

The room was spacious, uncluttered, with plush armchairs and an en suite bathroom with hotel-quality amenities. The bed, wide and adjustable, was layered with crisp linens and a cozy throw blanket I brought from home to use, making it feel more like a boutique hotel than a clinical space. Everything moved at a slower, more human pace – nurses came and went softly, the lighting dimmed, and the quiet was deep and restorative. It was a room made for healing, where exhaustion and joy could coexist in peace.

Once I settled into my cozy private room, I was able to have a few visitors. My precious lifelong friend Marie came to visit me shortly after I made it to the room. She sat at the far end of the hospital bed, and we spoke sweet words to one another. I was still quite out of it, yet her company warmed my heart.

"Adele, where is Akuma?" she asked.

"As far as I know he is in the NICU taking pictures of the babies for me. He has been gone for some time now," I stated with sadness.

Marie seemed dumbfounded by his absence. He was absent in every way that mattered, a hollow presence even when his name was spoken.

After the delivery nearly took my life, he didn't call, come to check up on me, he didn't show up in the recovery room, nor was he present when I arrived into the private room – not even once.

Soon after Marie left, my sweet friend, Charlotte from CCRM, who I had met at the IVF support group, had a few surprises for me. She burst into the room with two blue teddy bears and a pink teddy bear, and as she placed them in my lap, she too asked where Akuma was.

While I lay there trembling and pale in my hospital bed, stitched and bleeding and learning how to breathe again – Akuma carried on somewhere else, unreachable and unconcerned for my well-being.

How is it that my precious friends were happily waiting and counting down the minutes until they could come see me, visit with me, and bring me congratulatory gifts, and my own husband didn't think of buying me flowers, had no questions for me, no hand to hold in the sterile quiet of recovery.

His silence was deafening.

He was moving about as if nothing had happened.

All the while, I was clinging to life and the weight of it all – new motherhood, near death, and the sharp, aching realization I was utterly alone in a place he should have been by my side.

I found myself resting to the best of my ability, yet I was wondering where Akuma was as several hours had passed by. The babies were born at 10:42 a.m. and 10:43 a.m.; it was now close to four in the afternoon when Akuma walked into my hospital room.

My friend Charlotte sat at the end of the hospital bed, and Akuma took a chair next to my bed finally.

The surgical and nursing staff had all the bells and whistles set up for my continued recovery. I had compression cuffs placed on my legs to prevent blood clots and to increase circulation in my legs. The sleeves around my legs cycled continuously to tighten and release to keep the circulation ongoing.

"Ughhhh, I'm in so much pain. I need to call the nurse's station," I raptly mumbled.

"Oh, Del, are you okay? Is there something I can do to help you feel better?" Charlotte quickly asked.

"Ughh…ooohhh…can you please rub my legs and feet? Everything aches so much," I whimpered.

"Of course, I can."

"Thanks Charlotte."

Charlotte glanced over occasionally with much concern as to where Akuma was sitting in the chair as she consistently rubbed my legs and feet.

She began to think as questions pulsed through her mind like a second heartbeat: Are you seriously just sitting in the chair as Del lays here? Why aren't you offering to help her, go to the nurse's station for help? Why are you not even present for your wife? Not just physically, but in spirit, in soul, in care. He walked into the room and never even asked how she was doing, how she felt, he hadn't even touched her or held her hand. She literally just clawed her way back from the edge of something dark and final. Was he numb? A coward? Or just unwilling to see her broken and real? She had almost died bringing your children into the world, and you've treated her like an inconvenience, a disruption in your schedule. Was she asking too much – to be seen, to be loved, to not be invincible while her body and mind struggled to reassemble themselves?

Charlotte could bear no more. She turned her face away from Akuma and continued to focus on rubbing my legs and feet. She was no longer hoping he would intervene. She was disgusted with him.

I needed more assistance and pushed the red nurse's button attached to my bed. The nurse came in and asked me what I needed. I told her how uncomfortable I was and that I was feeling rather thirsty and hungry.

Charlotte noticed out of the corner of her eye once the nurse walked in, Akuma had placed his hand next to his ear and circled his pointer finger towards his ear, towards the nurse, as to show that Adele was crazy in her mind for asking for so much help from the nursing staff. It infuriated Charlotte so much, she mentioned to me she needed to go, and she left the room.

"Nurse, may I please have something to drink? I am so thirsty," I desperately asked.

"Adele, we need to wait a little bit longer until Dr. Patrick gives us the okay to move forward. You aren't out of the woods yet, and we need to make sure the bleeding continues to subside before we offer any liquids or solids," she insisted, "we need to make sure you don't have to return to the OR for a complete hysterectomy."

At the time, as I was laying bedside, I still had no feeling in my legs or in my toes, and I was watching Ice Age on TV to pass the time. I pushed the red button once more on my bed to get my nurse's attention again.

"Nurse, is there any chance I could get something to drink?" It was a quarter after four in the afternoon around this time when the nurse came back into my room.

"Not yet, Adele," she reminded me of the reason from before.

"Please...hey… look up at the TV. You know how the squirrel in Ice Age wants the nut?"

"Yeah, that movie is funny. The squirrel attempts many ways to get his paws on that nut in those movies," she laughed as she spoke.

"Yeah… I'm the squirrel today. Are you sure I cannot have a few sips of water?" I pleaded with her.

"Okay, Adele. I'll see what I can do about getting you some ice chips to start with," she kindly said.

About twenty minutes later she walked in with my nut, from Ice Age – a small Styrofoam cup of pellet-sized ice chips with a plastic spoon.

The first ice chip touched my tongue like a miracle – sharp, clean, impossibly cold. It melted slowly, flooding my dry mouth with a purity that tasted almost sweet. After more than several hours without food or water; it felt like my body had received a gift - each chip a moment of relief, of sensation, of being tethered back to the world. My lips were cracked, my throat raw, but the coldness soothed like silk on a sunburn. I let each chip melt completely before scooping up another, savoring the way the cool water slid down my throat, waking something quiet and parched inside of me. In that moment, it wasn't just hydration – it was comfort, reward, survival, distilled into tiny, glistening shards.

While enjoying my ice chips, I couldn't help but notice the eerie feeling of Akuma's lack of care towards me after my traumatic delivery.

Lying in my hospital bed, the sterile sheets tucked tightly around my body were more comforting then Akuma, who sat next to me scrolling through his phone, watching the TV, and staring blankly around the walls of the room.

I had almost died – almost left this world – and yet he wasn't truly there. He wouldn't touch me, nor would he ask if I was in pain, his eyes never met mine. I had thought that *that* kind of trauma would pull us closer together, make him see me in a new light – fragile, powerful, changed. But instead, he drifted farther away, as if my suffering bored him, as if my survival was just another item to ignore on his list. There was sadness, yes, but underneath it, something sharper: a betrayal that simmered just beneath the surface. Not loud, not screaming – but constant. How could he watch me fight my way back from the edge and remain so distant, so unmoved? In moments when I needed love to steady me, he gave me silence, and many times he mocked me. And that, more than the pain, more than the fear, was what truly hurt.

My first night after the delivery was met with much discomfort and perseverance. My night nurse Bettina was a fierce German woman who boldly told me what to do to help me recover physically.

"Alright, Mum, your vitals are all checked out. Would you like to try giving your first milk? Your colostrum? If you are able to get anything I can have it sent down to the NICU for your beautiful babies. Okay?" Bettina asked with her strong personality.

"Really? My body knows what to do that after all of this?" I inquired.

"Yes, Mum. You should be able to get something," she responded.

I was able to fill several small syringes of colostrum, and she called down to have the NICU retrieve the small vials of liquid gold.

"Okay, Mum. Get some rest, I will come back soon."

I was given oxycodone, ferrous sulfate, prenatal vitamins, and ibuprofen that evening to help with the pain and discomfort and to rebuild up the iron in my body after the continued blood loss.

"Alright, Mum, your vitals are all checked out again. Okay…we are going to try doing some movement, "Bettina insisted.

"Movement? What do you mean? I cannot even move my legs," I answered sharply.

"Yes, Mum. Our first goal is to get you to sit up from the bed in an upright position."

"Bettina, I don't think I can do this," I sullenly replied.

"Mum, let's give it a try," Bettina encouraged.

I looked at her like she was crazy, but I decided to give it a go.

Late into the early morning hours of October 26th, attempting to sit up after the surgery was the most trying event I can remember doing. It felt like scaling a mountain with nothing but raw willpower. Every muscle in my core screamed in protest, a deep searing pain that spread like fire through my midsection and lower back. I braced my arms, my hands gripped the sterile bed linens, until they turned a faint white. Sweat was already forming on my brow before I was able to move an inch. However, inch by inch, I lifted myself, breath hitching with each shift, as if my body was stitched together with threads too thin to hold.

It wasn't just pain – it was exhaustion, the kind that came from extreme blood loss, trauma, and sheer survival. My vision swam. My heart pounded, yet still I pushed, using every last shred of strength I could summon – not because I felt ready, but because I had to. I was climbing this mountain alone. Bettina and me. Me and Bettina.

Akuma never woke up; he never wanted to help me heal.

The moment I reached upright, hunched and trembling, the air hit my lungs like a cold slap, the tears pricked my eyes – not just from pain, but from the magnitude of it all. It was a fight. I had won that forty-five-minute climb at that moment.

"Good, Mum, you did great! Let's try again a little later," Bettina exclaimed.

"Again, later? You are out of your mind!" I breathlessly thought.

It must have been around three or four in the morning, when I was awakened again. Vitals checked and another visit from Bettina.

"Mum, we are going to work on something again. This time, I want you to sit up, swing your legs off the bed and walk over to this chair next to your hospital bed," Bettina commanded.

Lady, I don't know who you think I am or what I supposedly capable of doing, but all of that of what you just said – <u>that</u> is not happening.

I had a few choice words pop into my mind about what Bettina had in her agenda with this sitting up, swinging my legs over and walking to the chair, yet I knew "No" wasn't going to cut it with her.

Sitting up felt like tearing through layers of pain with nothing but grit. My arms shook as I pushed myself upright, the weight of my own body, especially my legs and feet, felt like a mountain pressing down on freshly stitched flesh. Every inch was fire – hot, tight, and unrelenting. The hospital gown clung damply to my back, and my breath came in shallow gasps as I slowly swung one leg off the side of the bed, then the other, my feet dangled just above the cold tile floor.

A strange warmth followed – a wetness pooling beneath me, trailing from the middle of the bed to the edge of it like something unraveling.

I glanced down. Blood. Everywhere. Dark, thick and vivid.

The blood dripped steadily from between my legs, painting the sterile white pad on top of the mattress in heavy blotches, a trail from what my body had endured.

I clenched my jaw and pressed my palms into the firm mattress, teeth gritted as I forced myself to stand. My knees buckled slightly, legs jelly-like and numb beneath me. The room tilted. The pain flared. But I moved.

Each step toward the chair was a battle – my hospital socks soaked through, my legs trembling under the weight of my blood loss and raw effort.

The blood kept falling, splashing softly on the floor behind me, leaving a path of breadcrumbs carved from my suffering. I reached the chair at last, collapsed near it, and let out a sound between a sob and a breath. I had moved only feet – but it had taken everything I had left.

I leaned on the chair briefly while Bettina called in more nurses to help clean up the bedding, lay down fresh linens, and an under pad to collect the blood that continued to leak out of me. She had the facilities manager assigned to the floor come clean up the blood puddles that had fallen below where I walked cautiously to the chair.

Bettina could see how exacerbated I had become and assisted me back to bed.

There was so much commotion going on post-op that my time spent with my miraculous babies was only from the brief glimpses I gave them before I began hemorrhaging in the OR. It was not until the afternoon of the 26th that I was allowed to take wheelchair transport to the NICU at the Rocky Mountain Hospital for Children next door to visit my newborn loves. My blood pressure had finally stabilized, and there were no preeclampsia symptoms. I was told the medical staff from the L&D floor had me on close surveillance, and they would make sure I was stable enough to move to the 11th floor for post-partum recovery.

My First Visit to the NICU

My new day nurse situated me in the wheelchair and explained that she would push me to the NICU, where I could visit my babies in the highest-level NICU, NICU III, known for the seriously ill and extremely premature babies who needed a high level of care. Akuma walked next to us as she wheeled me through PSL to RMHC.

The room was expansive and spacious; there was enough room in this ward to care for four babies. I was told Reece was on the far-left side, Kingston was on the left side closest to me and Scarlett was on the right side in the back. Reece weighed 2030 grams, Kingston 1795 grams and Scarlett 2210 grams. Shortly after delivery, Scarlett was on a C-PAP machine for about an hour due to the ingestion of some of the amniotic fluid. She was on the C-PAP to clear her lungs.

Akuma wheeled me next to Reece. He was so teeny and was crying when I first saw him. I recalled the sweet lullaby I sang to him while he grew and developed in utero. I began to sing it to him, and he stopped crying and looked right at me. It was such a breathtaking moment. Reece was so alert and recognized his mama's voice immediately.

I sat in the NICU III room in awe. I remember going over to each isolette, touching my babies' little torsos, and telling each of them how much I loved them. Once I saw Scarlett, I thought to myself, how did you all fit inside me? Each of you is so perfect. Ten fingers, ten little toes, and a sweet little frame of each of your bodies. Every feature, just perfect as God had planned. Now, they were so spread out…how did you all fit inside my womb? God is a God of miracles. Perfect little miracles.

The triplets were all on feeding tubes to gain nourishment. Reece, Kingston and Scarlet were all on room air on the day of their birth after Scarlett's stint with the C-PAP machine. Not one triplet needed oxygen to breathe. With the exception of their low birth weight, the triplets were extremely healthy, thriving, and cute.

My visit to the NICU was a short one, yet it was everything I waited years for. I needed to return to the L & D floor to be monitored and have my vitals checked again.

Recovery and Solitude

Early that evening, after a full 24 hours of surveillance had passed, I was given permission to move to the postpartum recovery floor. I was wheeled up to floor eleven and brought to room 11A. My legs were still very weak, and I could barely move them.

As soon as I saw the room I was moving into, after coming from the private room near the OR, I wanted to spread my legs wide eagle – the room was crooked, tiny, and it left me feeling as claustrophobic as I had pre-birth. I began to cry, and I couldn't believe I was being moved into this room. I began to have a panic attack, and many emotions flooded my mind.

"Akuma, I can't believe I have to recover in this room. It's so small. It's angled so weird, and it looks like it's old and worn down," I stated in an agitated way.

"I can't believe this is what I must sleep on. This chair looks and feels too uncomfortable," Akuma responded in the same, if not, more agitated way.

The night nurse asked if we wanted anything to eat for dinner. I was starving and so thrilled to be eating solid food again. I had my fill of ice chips for the past several hours, so this was like celebrating my own birthday. I ordered two BLT sandwiches with French fries and a cup of peppermint tea.

After eating dinner, the nurse checked my vitals again and sat down with Akuma and me to review postpartum recovery.

"Okay, Dad, you are going to help Mom walk around using the metal railing outside the recovery rooms. It's super important we get Mom up and moving to prevent post-operative pain from having her C-section and having her abdominal cavity open for the operation. This helps Mom heal, and it's vital to her recovery," she stated.

"I'm not doing that," Akuma interrupted.

"Yes, Dad, you are. You are going to help mom do this," she said more firmly.

"Adele, it's so important you keep drinking the peppermint tea. It will help heal a lot of the things you are dealing with. Dad, you will help Mom push her IV cart around, and Mom, you can use the metal railing to walk at a pace that is most comfortable for you," she explained, "also Mom, if things go well with you tonight – we'll let you shower in the morning."

Showering seemed like the next best reward after the ice chips, getting to see my beautiful babies, eating a great meal and now this. The smallest things brought me great joy at this point. I could hardly wait until tomorrow; my body had experienced so much trauma and the blood stains down my legs needed to be washed away. Nothing sounded better than a nice hot shower.

I got myself situated for the night and was waiting for Akuma to get his area ready for rest.

"Del, I'm not comfortable here. I'm going home," he said grimly.

"What do you mean you're leaving? You have to stay and help me recover; the nurse just told us…" I was rudely interrupted.

"I'm tired, dammit. I'm not staying here. Good night!" Akuma barked at me.

He gathered his belongings and stuffed everything in his overnight bag and walked abruptly out the door.

I immediately called my mom, bawling my eyes out. Telling her everything that had just happened and how he was supposed to help me walk around and assist me with my recovery. She couldn't believe her ears.

Yet, some twenty-five minutes later, he walked in our house where we shared the basement of my mom's walk out ranch house together.

My mom walked down to where he had just walked in and she screamed in his face, "*What* are you *doing here*? *Why* aren't *you* at the *hospital* with your *wife*?"

"I'm tired and I want to sleep. I am not getting any sleep down there. I don't want to be there. I'd rather be here to get some sleep," he said cowardly.

"Get your *ass* back down there. She needs you. What are you thinking? How can you be thinking of yourself after everything your wife just went through," my mom grimaced.

"Okay, fine. I'll go back," Akuma replied sheepishly.

The floor nurse had already done one round of walking with me around the recovery floor. She attempted to calm me down and help me focus on my recovery and not the sour actions of Akuma.

The next day was shower day, and I was looking forward to that. However, my first priority of the day was to get my wheelchair transport set up to visit Reece, Kingston and Scarlett.

Akuma offered to take me via wheelchair transport because he had made several trips to the NICU already. Because I was wheelchair-bound, I could not just go to the NICU at the drop of a dime. I was thankful Akuma wanted to take me. He hadn't been kind to me since I left the OR.

We had left the 11th floor via the elevator and traveled down to the main level to take a jig-jog to the entrance to RMHC. We were approaching a slight ramp before entering the jig-jog area, and Akuma began to push me up the ramp when he abruptly said, “I’m so sick of pushing you up this ramp. You are so fat and heavy.”

I sat there in my wheelchair, still tender and swollen from birth. My body marked by the trauma of my near-death hemorrhaging of losing more than 66% of blood volume in my body bringing our babies into this world. Stretch marks like lightning stretched across my belly and hips, my belly soft and heavy, healing, and healing slowly. My heart was still so raw, my emotions barely stitched together, where he made a comment like this, enough for others to hear.

His words were sharp, careless, tossed into the air like a joke: a jab at my weight, a comment about how “I really let myself go.”

My face flushed immediately, not from embarrassment, but from a cold kind of humiliation – that kind that sinks in deep, into the places that already hurt. I didn’t respond. I said nothing. I didn’t have words to say, not yet. My hands trembled slightly as I adjusted my hospital gown, as if to hide the evidence of what my body had done, of the miracles it had endured.

Akuma had seen me at my most vulnerable, my most powerful state – yet he still chose cruelty over care.

It was at this moment, with my heart aching and my body still recovering, I realized the deepest wound wasn’t the one healing in my abdomen – it was the one he had just opened with his words.

The abuse continued into every room I entered whether it was time spent sitting in the NICU with the triplets or in my own hospital room his words lingered like smoke- thin, toxic, impossible to escape. Even when he wasn't physically there, the echoes of his voice clung to the walls around me, following me from room to room like an invisible shadow.

In the NICU, where the machines hummed softly and the air was warm with hope, I should have felt reverence, peace, or something close to it. Instead, I heard him mockingly sing the lullaby I loved to sing to my loves in a consistent sarcastic annoying tone, criticizing me for sitting in the wheelchair rather than doing the cares NICU parent protocol where I would've had to stand to tend to the triplets to clean their eyes, check their temperature, feed the babies, and change their diaper. Akuma would roll his eyes at me as I tried to breastfeed. His voice wormed its way into every quiet moment, even over the rhythmic beeping of monitors and the rustle of nurses' scrubs.

When I finally made it back to my room, the floor nurse told me I could shower. Here was the moment I long awaited for – refreshment of the whole body and soul. I needed to continue to use a chair wherever I went. In bed, I was able to relax; however, whenever I wanted to go anywhere, I needed a wheelchair, and it was no different for me when taking a shower. The nurse had placed a shower chair in the bathtub and explained how to turn everything on.

Stepping into the hot shower two days after surgery felt like crossing into another world – one where healing didn't just mean stitches and medication, but warmth, comfort, and something close to relief. The first splash of water against my skin was almost too much – too hot, too alive – but then it melted into me like a healing balm. Steam curled around me, softening the air, wrapping me in a cocoon that felt safe for the first time in days.

The heat soothed my sore body, coaxing tension from my shoulders, neck, and back, down my spine; it was as if the water understood the weight I had carried. It ran gently down and began to wash away my blood-stained legs and crevices where the hemorrhage occurred.

With each droplet that slid down my back, I felt more human again – less like a patient, more like me. It was all so simple, but after pain and stillness, it felt luxurious and sacred. After being surrounded by beeping machines, the blood, and the fear – disappeared. There was only the water, the warmth, and the quiet reminder: I made it through. I'm still here.

Unfortunately, this sacred time was interrupted by Akuma telling me to get out of the shower because I had been there too long, according to his standards.

The weight of Akuma's contempt was always there – pressing down on my shoulders, filling my chest with shame. His cruelty was precise – measured in looks, silences, and sharp quiet sentences that left bruises where no one could see.

I tried to breathe, tried to heal, but the air felt dense with everything he'd say – the way he scoffed at my pain, dismissed me, rolled his eyes when I cried or needed extra help from the nurses on the postpartum floor.

His dismissive behavior intensified as he chose to leave every night from the second day forward not to be at my bedside during recovery.

Even the walls at night felt complicit, like they'd absorbed his disdain and were now breathing it back at me. I was never alone, not really. His presence haunted the space, not through care or concern, but through the way his words had rooted themselves inside of me.

Recovery should've been sacred. Instead, it was shadowed – each moment of rest broken by the memory of his voice telling me I wasn't enough. Even when I closed my eyes, his words followed me there too.

Those nights I spent alone recovering from the post-cesarean surgery caused immense back and neck pain that was so severe I could barely breathe. It felt impossible to inhale and sit upright, let alone lean back against my bed. Much of my time at night was spent trying to figure out how to breathe; while it felt like someone was stabbing a butcher knife into all the nerves connecting my head to my neck and shoulders.

On October 28th, I was able to get my catheter removed. I was still on close surveillance due to the hemorrhage. Unfortunately, a new concern developed overnight as transaminases spiked within those 24 hours from the day before.

I was told the day before I could be potentially be discharged on October 29th if everything continued to improve and I was able to continue my checklist of postpartum "to do's" that were on the wall of my hospital room. Items such as – passing gas, having a stool movement, completing the birth certificate worksheet, and setting up follow-up care once I leave the hospital to name a few.

However, with the spike in transaminases discovered from a blood prick test, the medical staff discovered my liver enzymes may have been damaged from the hemorrhage. This condition may have been affected when I experienced class IV Trauma-Hemorrhagic Shock due to losing over three liters of blood. I was told I may need to stay in the hospital for an additional four days.

The supervision and surveillance intensified that day. I was receiving blood pricks often, and my blood pressure continued to be checked regularly every few hours. I was on several medications to help with pain management, to control the bleeding, iron medication to build my body back up, and medicine to lower the edema caused due to swelling. Now that the catheter was removed, every time I used the bathroom, I used a fracture bedpan to measure the output of everything in my bladder.

I felt like a lab rat – poked, prodded, and measured.

After the surgery and the complications that followed, my body no longer felt like my own. It belonged to the parade of doctors, nurses, and specialists who entered my room with clipped voices and sterile hands, lifting sheets, checking incisions, adjusting machines, and scribbling notes as if I were a case file instead of a human being.

IVs were switched out like parts on a machine, blood drawn again and again until my fingers were painted with tender burns. Even my pain felt like data – numbers on a chart, something to be managed, observed, but never fully acknowledged for what it truly was.

I wanted to be seen – not just scanned.

Heard – not just monitored.

But in that room, where Akuma would mysteriously appear – I was just a patient. A vessel. A subject to be studied and in those quiet moments between check-ins, I wondered if he even remembered my name.

My only oasis was the time I spent in the NICU with my babies. I was told the babies had graduated from NICU III to NICU II in a day and a half. Their status was improving greatly. Reece had moved from a feeding tube to his first bottle and was officially off IV fluids on the 28th of October. Kingston also had his first bottle thirty minutes after Reece. Scarlett, Kingston, and Reece were all in room air in the NICU and Scarlett received her first bottle at noon that same day.

The NICU was the one place where everything else seemed quiet, where the pain in my body and the chaos outside the doors faded into something softer.

After being wheeled down to the NICU into that dim, warm, and sterile triplet ward, everything seemed less sharp, softened by the rhythmic beeping of baby monitors, and the fragile, sacred presence of new life. In that space, I wasn't just a patient recovering from surgery and hemorrhage. I was a mother.

Even in my wheelchair, stitched and exhausted, I found a strength I didn't know I had. I'd cradle their tiny hands, hold them and sing to them, speak gently over the sound of the machines, my voice trembling, but steady – because here, I had purpose. Here, my broken body didn't define me. I breastfed, adjusted their blankets, memorized every feature – the curve of their cheek, their smell, their tiny features, the rise and fall of their chests. The pain didn't disappear, but it bent to the background, overshadowed by the fierce, quiet devotion that welled up deep inside me.

The NICU became a sanctuary. Not because it was free from fear, but because it was filled with love – raw, overwhelming, life-giving love. In those hours beside their cribs, even in a wheelchair, stitched and bleeding, I felt more whole than I had anywhere else.

"Hi, Ms. Charles, I'm Piper. I am your triplets' primary care nurse. It's so nice to meet you. I have heard you have gone through quite the ordeal during delivery. Please know you do not have to use the cares protocol until you are well enough to do so. I am happy to help you move from your wheelchair to one of the recliners and if you want to breastfeed one of your babies I can set everything up for you and hand him or her to you. Only do what you want or are capable of – you will have plenty of days to diaper and feed your babies," Piper happily shared.

Piper was more than a nurse. She was a lifeline woven into the hardest, most vulnerable days of my life. From the moment I first wheeled into the NICU, fragile and aching, she met me not just with professionalism, but with a fierce, unwavering compassion that wrapped around me like a safety net. She cared for my triplets as if they were her own – gentle hands tending to their delicate bodies, soft whispers soothing their cries, steady presence anchoring them in a world of wires and whirring machines.

But she didn't stop at them. She saw me. The mother behind the wheelchair, behind the pain and the exhaustion. She remembered my name, noticed when I was too quiet, and never once made me feel like a burden. She taught me how to hold my babies, how to feed them, how to feel like a mother again when everything in my body still felt broken.

There was a grace in her care, a mix of skill, heart, and intuition that turned the walls of the NICU into a space where love could still bloom. In a season filled with worry, she gave me moments of peace, dignity, and hope. I will never forget the way she spoke to my babies with tenderness or how she encouraged me, piece by piece, to believe I could do this. She didn't just care for my children – she helped heal me.

"Hi, this is Piper...oh, yes…she is here in the NICU ward…oh, uh-huh…okay, I will let her know. Thanks bye. Hey Adele, you are needed upstairs again to get your blood test and your pressure checked. The floor nurse has been looking for you for a while. I will schedule your wheelchair transport to get you back to your floor," she kindly explained.

After days of fierce observation, the liver enzymes stabilized, my oxygen levels were above 96%, the bleeding had lessened dramatically, my body was able to pass gas and have regular loose stools, my iron was gaining steadily, my incision was healing well, and all the bells and whistles checked off miraculously. I had officially graduated from postpartum recovery and was discharged from the hospital.

I was told to follow a strict protocol when I left the hospital: do not lift anything heavier than my baby or do any kind of strenuous activity, limit walking and moving, no driving allowed, and I was told to continue to use a wheelchair for the next month to get around. I still did not have the strength to stand. At most, I could stand for roughly thirty seconds before the feelings of passing out would occur.

Returning Home

Coming home from the hospital was a time to return to safety and rest. Most importantly, a place to feel the love of my mom. After the long, harrowing days at PSL mostly solo, and carrying the weight of physical pain, emotional exhaustion, and the hollow absence of support from my husband, I knew being home with my mom would make my worries fade.

The front yard had "Welcome Home" baby carriage signs staked gently in the grass, with two blue, "It's a boy" and one pink, "It's a girl" signs. The seasoned trees with their brilliant oranges, reds and yellows welcomed fall; it was as if the earth itself was celebrating my strength and survival.

Fresh, soft pink blooming roses lined with baby's breath filled a vase in my kitchen, and its scent met me before the door did. It was as if my mother had tried to outshine the sterile air of the hospital with beauty, color, and warmth.

When I stepped inside, the air was different. It didn't carry the piercing edge of cold detachment or unspoken resentment – it was warm, gentle. There was food on the stove being prepared of a home-cooked favorite, slow-cooked, familiar, nourishing in ways beyond hunger. Each meal, words spoken, and thoughtful action felt like a love letter written in spices and her compassion.

My mom's presence was a healing balm to my weary soul. She wrapped me in the kind of care that saw my pain, didn't question my silence, and held me in it without judgement. She saw the invisible bruises – the loneliness, the betrayal, the absence of a partner who should have stood by my side – and answered them with her presence. Constant, quiet, unyielding presence.

She didn't need me to explain the distance my husband kept or how his absence felt like abandonment dressed up as indifference. She saw the hurt that lingered in my eyes, even as I smiled for my babies. Instead of asking why or demanding more from me, she simply gave. She gave her hands, her feet, her time, patience, food, and her home. In her refuge, for the first time in five days, I was allowed to simply be: a woman healing, a mother recovering, a soul grieving and growing all at once.

The triplets were still in NICU II under the supervision of several wonderful doctors and nurses, and in the next numerous days, the following occurred: phototherapy, skin to skin contact, Scarlett's first smile at four days old, Reece wearing his first onesie at four days old, the nurses' dressed the triplets up for Halloween, Reece outgrew his preemie onesie at five days old, Reece and Kingston had their circumcision surgery. We were told on October 29th to expect the triplets to be in the NICU for up to four to six weeks, but God had other plans.

NICU Graduations

Reece was set to graduate from the NICU to come home on November 7th, just thirteen days after delivery, because he was able to do the following: consistently gain weight for a week's time, eat everything on his own without using a feeding tube, maintain his temperature outside of the isolette, and breathe without any apneas or Bradycardic episodes – meaning he didn't stop breathing or have a drop in his heart rate for five days consistently. He also had to pass a four-hour car seat test to ensure that he could maintain the correct position and oxygenation for the duration of the car ride home.

Knowing Reece would be coming home on November 7th, we were told to get everything ready for his arrival. My NICU nurse, Piper, told me to get our Christmas decorations up the night before we were to bring him home. She said I would be too tired to do much else, so the evening of November 6th, we set up the Christmas decorations along with a seven-foot-tall Christmas tree lined with colored lights.

The NICU II staff wanted to make sure every parent felt at ease and prepared for the journey home. It was customary for every parent to spend the night on the NICU floor in one of two private rooms to stay in a fully equipped room with monitors, a crib or isolette, a queen-sized bed, a recliner, and all the supplies nurses taught you to use for a full twelve hours unattended by the medical staff.

The goal in this autonomous venture was to be fully confident in bringing the baby home for in-home care. Thankfully, none of the triplets had ongoing medical needs of breathing difficulties, feeding issues, infections, long-term developmental delays, or congenital anomalies. The only concerns were their low birth weight, born six weeks early, and how to continue to increase more calorie intake and weight.

I felt prepared and ready to take on this responsibility. Each day since my delivery, my body continued to heal. Even though I was still limited as I arrived at the NICU in wheelchair transport, I knew I could do this. I was a self-proclaimed night owl and I was his mother, of course I could do this.

"Good afternoon, Mr. Campbell and Ms. Charles. We have you all checked into room two for your 12-hour stay with Reece. Congratulations to both of you for making it this far in your NICU journey. Come on in, we have everything set up for you – Reece's crib, extra blankets, extra pacifiers, a bottle warmer, bottles, and formula. The room is equipped with a queen-size bed, recliner, and a fully equipped bathroom for your needs. The goal over the next twelve hours is to do this on your own and not have to call the nurse's station for assistance, but if you are experiencing a medical emergency, we are just outside the door. We will wheel Reece in from the triplet ward where his brother and sister are, so you can get started and settled."

"Wow, this looks so nice. I love that the NICU does this!" I exclaimed.

"The nurse said none of the monitors will make noise, thank goodness," Akuma commented.

"I think it's to help us know what to do," I responded.

"Okay, so how do you want to do this?" Akuma asked.

"How about we take turns every feeding? That way we can both rest. How does that sound?" I suggested.

"That works, I call second shift," Akuma replied.

That first night alone with Reece was like stepping into a world where time slowed down, emotions ran high, and everything ordinary became extraordinary.

I took the time to gently lay Reece down in his crib after a bottle feeding and did all the tasks we learned in the care protocol – clean his eyes, take his temperature and if needed, change his diaper.

Even though I had done this over and over in the NICU prior, there was a newness to everything. My heart pounded, unsure if I was doing everything right and fully aware it was all real. The room felt quieter than usual, yet every sound Reece made amplified my senses. I listened wide-eyed as he breathed, light, quick, and perfect.

I was caught between awe and alertness, unable to fully fall asleep when it was my time to rest because I couldn't get over the fact that I was going to get to do this for the rest of my life, being Reece's mother.

Sleep came in whispers, I'd blink at it'd be 10:00 p.m., then 12:17 a.m., then 2:00 a.m., 3:45 a.m., then 4:51 a.m., and finally close to 7:00 a.m.. Sleep interrupted by tiny grunts, cluster feeds, diaper changes, and repositioning.

I was awake, feeling delirious, half-dreaming, sitting upright in the recliner holding Reece doing skin-to-skin. My body was screaming for rest, but my mind wouldn't stop ticking through the mental checklists: Is he okay? I think last night went well. Thank goodness I'm a night owl. Did

I swaddle him right? Did I burp him enough? Even in the depths of fatigue, I marveled at the miracle I made in my womb.

That quiet moment of holding Reece next to me in the early morning hour of November 7th was such a golden moment. Skin to skin. Heartbeat to heartbeat. A time I could never forget.

"So, how do you think last night went?" Akuma asked.

"I thought it went rather well. I think we worked well as a team taking turns," I responded with joy. I needed to reposition myself while I held Reece in the recliner, so I was taking my time to readjust and position Reece on my opposite arm when I accidentally dropped the pacifier and it fell onto the tile floor below.

"Well, I was going to give you an A for your effort and time spent with Reece last night, but after you dropped the pacifier on the floor and are making me pay for that additional pacifier below his crib, I'm going to give you a grade of a B minus," he rudely said to me.

"Wow, a grade? You are giving me a grade now? You have got to be kidding me," I griped.

Our time in the NICU's private room came to an end and we managed to make it the whole twelve hours without needing assistance and with that, Reece's discharge papers began being processed.

With time to wait as several things needed to be done and processed before we could take our bundle of joy home, I urgently made a visit to the NICU nurse station to share what had just occurred with Akuma.

"Good morning, Nurse Jennah. I just had a bizarre thing happen to me while being in room two. My husband gave me a grade on how well I took care of my son this morning and I find it odd, don't you?" I asked with great concern. "He has been acting so strange with me since the delivery with the triplets. He has been distant, verbally abusive, and downright mean. Is there any way he can see one of the psychologists before we leave with Reece? I wonder if he has male postpartum depression. I mean…that can happen in men, right? Because I can't understand why he is acting like this."

"Yes, it can happen. And yes, I find it bizarre that he would give you a grade. Let me reach out to our psychologist and I'll see what we can do," she informed me.

Reece's First Night Home – November 7, 2014

My first night home with Reece was sacred. I moved from so much anticipation, from painstaking infertility, to IVF appointments, biweekly OB appointments, NICU visits, and finally to the reality of bringing home my first-born son. The dreams of who he might be washed over me and into the overwhelming presence of who he is.

Akuma carried him through the back door for the first time in his little bucket car seat. His head barely peeked up above the five-strap harness. Reece was such a little guy.

The nursery had been ready for months. The walls were painted a stormy gray. His crib, untouched until now, had been hand-picked with white and soft grey cozy crib sheets. The glider was positioned in the room next to all three cribs.

Reece's bedding was soft grey and white, Kingston's was bold navy and white, and Scarlett's was splashes of purple and white. The baby monitor was set up, the drawers filled with neatly folded onesies, and a nearby closet filled with stacks and stacks of diapers and wipes.

Reece was trained to eat every four hours, so that first night home we were busy watching, feeding, holding, changing, whispering, checking and double-checking. We moved through the hours in a strange, beautiful haze, guided by love and adrenaline. Every cry set my heart racing. Every quiet stretch I found myself gazing at his beautiful soul. I kissed him about a dozen times, maybe more. I held onto him just a little longer each time.

I would whisper promises in the dark, words only meant for his ears. "I'm here, Reecy. I love you. I've been waiting for you." I repeatedly sang the lullaby *Baby Love* written by Nicole C. Mullen and only changed the words to my children's names. It always lulled him to sleep. "Reecy, you are mama's precious little boy…Reecy, you always bring me so much joy…and I'm so glad God gave you to me…sleepy angel…face of peace…and I'm so glad, God gave you to me…now close your eyes and go to sleep."

Restrictions with Premature Babies

We were on strict orders since being in the NICU and had several recommendations on how to help our preemies grow and develop. It was vital to their continued growth and development to pay close attention to the babies being over-stimulated and overwhelmed by transitioning home. This was a list of the recommendations for preemies who spent time in NICU care and more in particular during cold and flu season during the 1st and 2nd week at home:

- Limit the number of visitors to only familiar people – parents, siblings, and grandparents only.
- Keep the environment quiet and somewhat dim – providing some day/night cycling.
- Provide swaddling and boundaries during positioning and handling
- When feeding, **do not** have any distractions i.e. radio, TV, conversations, rocking
- Sleep patterns are very important and should not be interrupted. **Do not pick up a sleeping baby** just to hold them. Holding should occur during caregiving times, or when the baby is awake.

After the first two weeks at home:

- Continue to limit visitors, allowing only 1 – 2 visitors at a time. Limiting this to close family friends (support people) and direct family members.
- **Only parents or direct care givers should handle** the baby during visiting. (Remember, your baby is still premature.) Preterm infants often become disorganized and over-stimulated when passed from person to person.
- Continue to monitor the environment, introducing one new stimulus at a time.
- It is OK to place the baby in an infant seat or swing for up to 20 minutes.
- If the weather permits, taking a walk outside can be beneficial, making sure to stay within five minutes of your home. (Dress the baby appropriately depending on the weather and always protecting the baby from direct sunlight.)

For the first month after discharge:

- Large crowds are not recommended – i.e. church, grocery stores, malls, restaurants…remember that your baby was born early and has spent an extended time in the neonatal intensive care unit and it is strongly recommended that your baby is not exposed to any young children, with the exception of siblings, secondary to the risk for infection and illness.

Because of Cold and Flu Season:

- Use all of the above restrictions and continue them from November through April.

Other advice given while at the NICU was to reduce light, reduce noise and do not rock your baby. The overstimulation of any of this would cause the preemie to lose weight and calories and could potentially be dangerous or harmful to our children.

While I was thrilled to bring my babies home from the NICU, I also struggled with the torn relationship and strain on my marriage. I never heard anything back from Nurse Jennah about getting Akuma in to see a counselor, and it was something I ended up dealing with on my own. I was willing to do everything to keep my babies healthy, yet due to the strongly recommended restrictions, I struggled with the thought of silence, non-communication, and the utter darkness I was to endure from November to April.

Scarlett's Graduation – November 8, 2014

Scarlett was sent home the following day after Reece on Saturday, November 8th from the NICU. I thought I had this parenting thing under my belt, as I had mentioned before of being a "night owl". This was a whole other level in its own way. I tread slowly after this first night home with Scarlett. The next day, roughly mid-morning, I was an emotional wreck.

Where is my phone? Oh my gosh…it's already 11:00 in the morning? Seriously? I never ate dinner last night after Scarlett came home. I still haven't eaten breakfast…ugh… where is my phone…Reece is crying…Scarlett is crying… I'm blazing exhausted…ugh, I still haven't pumped for the bottle…my eyes… my eyes…my eyes… are burning…how am I going to do this tonight…I need to rest…wait, what was I looking for? What was I going to do? Hmmm…oh, yeah…where is my phone? There it is under the glider…oh my gosh…the diaper pail…oh, gross, what is that? What was I doing? Oh yeah, I have this brilliant idea. I am going to send a text message to everyone on my phone. Yes! That's it. Here is what I will say…let's see here…Good Morning Everyone…Two of the triplets are home as of the past few days and I need some help. So…yeah… that looks great…so, I am wondering if any of you give to a charity or if you give to several charities, would you please consider giving to me? I need help with the babies. Could you drop by sometime this week and help me?

Yes…this looks good and desperate. Because, yes, I am desperate. I need to send out this S.O.S – save our sister. Yes, this is brilliant…okay, how many contacts…hmmm… let's just send to all of them. Yes, even more convincing. Text Message sent…text message sent…text message sent… waiting…waiting…only one response.

At the time of the text, it was a Sunday morning and most of my extended family was at church – my mom, my sister Aster and her husband Sam.

Beep.

Simultaneous beep.

Beep.

"Hey, Mom, did you just get a text from Adele?" Aster whispered.

"Yes, I believe so," she responded.

"Ast, I just got one too," Sam exclaimed.

My sister got the biggest kick out of this S.O.S. report and declaration of desperation. Growing up together, she has always known me from the ripe age of three to me saying, "I will do it!" Basically, she knew I loved being an independent woman with an agenda I created and would usually complete myself.

"Ms. Independent needed desperate help," and she laughed at my expense.

Kingston's Graduation – November 11, 2014

Kingston came home from the NICU on Tuesday, November 11th. This is where strength of mind, body, spirit and soul coexist. Nothing could have prepared me for three babies at home in record time from the hospital. The triplets spent less than three weeks in the neonatal intensive care unit and were home. I did receive good help from my dear sister Aster and my mom during that time where only immediate family should be present.

Motherhood and triplets were an around-the-clock job.

The epitome of exhaustion caring for triplet preemies is something words can barely touch – you live it, moment by moment, breath by breath. It's not just being tired – it's a complete unravelling of your physical, emotional, and mental reserves, all in service of keeping three fragile lives afloat.

You are never not needed.

The days blur into nights, and nights dissolve into dawn. Each day is marked by a cycle of feeds, diaper changes, pumping, cleaning, soothing, watching, worrying – and repeat. There's no such thing as rest between tasks, because by the time you finish with baby A, baby B is crying, and just as you settle baby B down, baby C spits up or won't settle unless being held.

Those first few days were brutal when Kingston came home because on NICU time, they were on all different feeding times –

Reese ate at 8:00 a.m., 11:00 a.m., 2:00 p.m., 5:00 p.m., 8:00 p.m., 11:00 p.m., 2:00 a.m., 5:00 a.m. – repeat.

Kingston ate at 8:30 a.m., 11:30 a.m., 2:30 p.m., 5:30 p.m., 8:30 p.m., 11:30 p.m., 2:30 a.m., 5:30 a.m. – repeat.

Scarlett ate at 9:00 a.m., 12:00 p.m., 3:00 p.m., 6:00 p.m., 9:00 p.m., 12:00 a.m., 3:00 a.m., 6:00 a.m. – repeat.

When did I sleep?

I think I went for a solid 72 hours with little to no sleep. My body operated on auto-pilot – hands moving by memory, legs swaying with minimal thought as I was still recovering from my C-section, eyes half-lidded, but always alert. I was sleep deprived to the point of being nauseated. Delusions flicker at the edges of my vision. I cry over spilled milk – literally – because every drop pumped feels like a miracle I worked too hard to lose.

I couldn't remember the last time I ate a hot meal, drank water, brushed my teeth, took a shower, or heard silence. My muscles ached. I was constantly listening for sounds the babies made.

My living space felt like a battlefield. Twenty-seven bottles to fill every day. Formula to mix. The dishwasher ran every 24 hours. Laundry never ended. I smelled like coffee, soap, breast milk, formula, and tears, yet there was no place I would rather be because this is what I prayed for.

And furthermore – I loved them more fiercely than I ever thought possible. Even in my lowest moments, sitting on the chair too exhausted to move, my eyes burning from lack of sleep – I still reached for them. I continued to show up. Again, and again. I held the line between life and chaos.

This is exhaustion that reshapes you. Not just in body, but in soul. I am not the person I was before they arrived – I am someone more tender, more raw, more powerful, more undone.

And though my body went through so much trauma – my spirit – somehow holds. Because these babies, these tiny warriors, are watching me, depending on me, and they are worth every sleepless night, every stretch mark, and every shattered nerve.

Late into the evening of November 13th, Akuma oversaw putting Kingston down after his bottle close to midnight. It was vital to the triplets' continued growth to also have the room warmed to 68 – 73 degrees Fahrenheit, to wear a knit cap since 80% of body heat is lost through the head, and to always have one extra layer when sleeping through the night i.e. using a onesie along with a tucked and tightened swaddled blanket.

During cares in the NICU, having a body temperature of 97.7 – 99 degrees Fahrenheit or 36.5 – 37.22 degrees Celsius was in the normal range for preterm babies. Up until the triplets reached their actual due date of December 5th, we were to continue to follow this same norm.

When it was my shift to oversee Kingston at his next feeding, he had woken up before his "scheduled" feeding of 2:30 am about an hour and a half beforehand, screaming. Something didn't seem right, and I attempted to move faster than my body would allow.

"Oh, Kingston, what's wrong, buddy?"

I noticed he was showing signs of stress from the NICU sheets we had discussed with Piper before being discharged.

Somehow, he wasn't swaddled at all, and he was exposed to too much air. Kingston was pale and white, his breathing changed, and he was limp in his limbs, neck, face, and trunk. I notified my mom and Akuma that something was seriously wrong with Kingston. I gathered a few things in my diaper bag and had Akuma place the bucket seat in the back of the car to rush him to the nearest Emergency Department.

When we arrived at the ED at 2:04 am, the doctor took Kingston's temperature, and it showed an extremely low reading at 35.0 and 35.1 degrees Celsius or 95 degrees Fahrenheit.

As a pre-term baby, this was dangerously low and considered hypothermia. Lab work was completed and everything came back normal, thankfully. We were sent home on strict orders to snuggle up with lots of blankets and to cuddle for the rest of the day near the warm hearth, blazing with fire.

Providing Additional Hands

The following week was a turning point.

Still raw from delivery and tender from surgery, I found myself leaning harder than ever on my mom and my sister. Without hesitation, Aster rallied beside me – her presence steady, her love fierce. Together we stepped into a rhythm of round-the-clock care for the triplets.

My mom still worked full-time and opted to help with the early morning shift from five o'clock in the morning to 6:30 am before she had to be at work at seven o'clock sharp.

Akuma and I took turns switching in the middle of the night. I helped during the day when I could, as I still needed to rest and not do too much strenuous work, and my sister helped every day after she had dropped her girls off at school and until close to pick up at three o'clock in the afternoon. Feedings, diaper changes, soothing cries throughout the day – it was an exhausting dance, but one we were all committed to.

Akuma's Unpredictable Behavior

What had started as a concern quickly moved into undeniable clarity: my husband was unraveling. At first, it was subtle – missed feedings he promised to handle, not letting me pump for milk, complaining about getting up – to times he would leave once someone came down to help – my mom of all people.

He would leave in the middle of a task, with excuses that never added up. His absence grew louder than his presence. His words became hollow – promises made in the morning were broken by nightfall. He withdrew emotionally, avoided the babies, avoided me – he became unpredictable, sometimes volatile. There was an edge to his tone that hadn't been there before, a bitterness that felt misplaced in our fragile new world.

The red flags multiplied.

He'd lash out when gently confronted, claiming victimhood in moments when the babies needed him the most. His frustration wasn't with the challenge of newborns – it was with the expectation to show up; when he did show up, it was often for performance, not presence.

My sister saw it too. There was a quiet understanding between us, an unspoken pact forged during feeding times and long looks exchanged while washing bottles or changing diapers. Aster didn't question my intuition; she fortified it. Together, we began to build a protective shell around the babies – and around me. Her support wasn't just practical; it was emotional armor. She became my co-parent, my backup, my sanity. Through sleep-deprived days and tearful nights, she stood next to me – for the babies, for me. Slowly and painfully, the truth became clearer. The man who should have been my partner was becoming a danger to my peace. The weight of this realization was heavy – for days, weeks, hours, and minutes to come.

About a week later, after my sister had dropped off her girls to come and help, she found me in a puddle of tears, alone with the babies, and Akuma was nowhere to be seen.

"Where is Akuma?" Aster inquired.

"I don't know. He got up at 6:30 in the morning and just left. He didn't tell me where he was going or when he'd be back, and his phone is turned off," I cried profusely. "I am not supposed to be doing all the lifting, and I've been sitting here for the past three hours doing it all alone."

"Oh my gosh, Delly!" Aster voiced. "What the hell is wrong with him?"

"I don't know. Something is so wrong with him, though. I tried to schedule something with the hospital staff. I made so many complaints to my postpartum nurses and the NICU staff. All I can think of is postpartum male depression. I mean…I get that it's a lot. Three babies, yet he knew all along for several months what we were getting into. He was so supportive all throughout the pregnancy and all throughout IVF. He came to *every* appointment, and now, I don't know what this is…I don't know who he is anymore," I explained.

Aster canceled her plans for the day, rearranged her schedule, and helped me until nine o'clock in the evening to make sure I was safe.

Akuma made his appearance around dinner time. Aster was near the door's entrance helping clean up while I was in the room resting when he walked through the back door.

"Oh, hi, Aster," Akuma uttered.

"Where have *you been* all day? Do you realize you left her here by herself while she is only weeks out from her traumatic birth, and to top it off, three preemies? What the heck were you thinking?" she barked.

"Well, you see...Del told me to leave and told me not to come back until dinner time...she kicked me out," he lied aloud.

"Akuma, that is pathetic. Adele would not have kicked you out when she clearly was depending on you to help with the babies, as she is limited in her own ability to lift and manage things on her own. *You are such a liar*!" she snapped.

Akuma had nothing more to say and walked sheepishly away as he continued to avoid Aster until she left later that night.

In the weeks that followed the birth of our triplets, my husband – the person I thought would be my partner in this journey – continued to pull away from his responsibilities. Not in a momentary way, but in a deep, intentional absence. He made it a regularity to disappear with every excuse in the book to get out of feedings, diaper changes, comforting cries, helping with bottles and laundry – tasks he promised to help with – were suddenly my responsibilities alone. If I asked for help, it was met with sighs, eye rolls, or silence. And worse – sometimes, I was met with words that cut.

The verbal abuse crept in slowly at first, like poison diluted in water. He'd say things like: you don't know how to be a mother, I never wanted these babies in the first place, I hate when your mom comes down here – I feel like I have two wives, I bought you an outfit – its XXXL because that's how fat you are, you shouldn't eat that cake Nurse Piper made – you definitely don't need that, I cannot believe you are getting all of the attention – what about me? Why don't you do the whole night shift by yourself, so I can sleep? Maybe if you weren't so lazy, I'd feel like helping, you care more about the triplets than me.

What he had said to me was so icy and cold, it stung. He didn't just refuse to help; he made me feel guilty for needing help in the first place. I was healing from childbirth, emotionally vulnerable, and doing everything I could to keep our babies' fed, warm, and safe – yet he made me feel like a failure for not doing more.

His presence became another weight I carried – one heavier than the exhaustion, heavier than the newborn cries, heavier than the demands of motherhood itself. I found myself tiptoeing around his moods, avoiding asking for anything, and swallowing my needs just to keep the peace. Instead of being my partner, he became a source of tension, fear, and emotional harm.

Wellness Visit

It was the triplets' one-month wellness visit on November 26, 2014. Akuma made me carry the bucket seats up to the doctor's office on my own. The kids all received their shots, got weighed, and measured. I had always carried a notebook with me to track everything that occurred from each well visit, calls to the doctor, medical information, and information from their NICU care. A trait I loved about myself was how organized I was and how detailed I was with information.

"Adele, put that down and come help with Scarlett," Akuma glowered at me.

"I will, just as soon as I write down what Reece's results were," I calmly responded.

"Get over here! She is about ready to get her shots," Akuma hissed.

"It's okay, Akuma. We have extra NPs to help. We know this is a lot for mom and family to endure," the doctor interrupted.

What the heck is your problem? Gosh, I want to write this down. Give me a second. For goodness' sake, there are five additional people here to help. Give me a break!

The wellness visit took roughly an hour to complete and then it was time to get ready to go.

"Okay, let's do this. Let's place the babies all together, lined up in this spacious area away from other patients waiting for their appointments in the waiting room, to keep them safe and to continue to follow the recommendations from the NICU for at-home care," the doctor announced.

"Akuma, why don't you head out and pull up the car in front of our practice, so it's easier to get the triplets to the car," a nurse practitioner suggested.

As soon as Akuma had left and was out of sight, the pediatrician and her nurse practitioner pulled me aside.

"Adele, are you being abused at home?" they both asked earnestly.

"He has been very distant and verbally abusive to me," I shared.

"It looks like it. I didn't like the way he spoke to you during the wellness visit. Please keep us informed of anything you are concerned with," they agreed.

"Here…I am going to give you my personal cell number. Call or text if you ever have an emergency," the doctor said, concerned.

"I see him; he is coming out of the elevator," the NP warned.

"Alright, guys, the babies are all bundled up and ready to go. Enjoy your first Thanksgiving tomorrow, and we'll see you at the end of December for the triplets' two-month wellness visit," they said warmly.

Our First Thanksgiving

Akuma's irresponsible and reckless behavior towards our family made our first Thanksgiving together memorable, and not in a great way. With only one month and a few days post-birth, my sister was hosting the holiday celebration, and everyone was invited to come, as usual.

However, as had happened so many times before, I ended up coming alone to the holiday meal, fully responsible for all three babies and all the gear necessary for the triplets: car seat carriers, the diaper bag, bottles, swaddling blankets, pacifiers – you name it, I had it with me. I wasn't supposed to be lifting anything over five pounds, but I definitely was lifting it all.

Akuma could never quite tell me what his reason was for not coming, but it was becoming more wearying for me. All of his behavior and the horrible attitude he had was taking a toll on my well-being.

A Gift to Lift Me Up

My mom knew I was down in the dumps about the abusive treatment and the exhaustion of all of the newborn duties, so amid it all – newborn life and recovery – my mom showed up in a way only a mother can – with a quiet kind of magic and deep, intuitive love. She could see it all in my eyes: the fatigue, the worry, the weight I was carrying, so, she did what she always does best – she found a way to lift me up.

One afternoon, as I sat curled up on the couch in between feedings, still in my spit-up-on pajamas and clutching a lukewarm cup of coffee, she surprised me with the gentlest smile and said, "I booked you a gift, a newborn photo shoot at home." She wasn't just giving me pictures. She was giving me permission to pause and celebrate, to see the beauty I was too tired to notice, and to remind me that even in chaos, this moment mattered.

As the camera clicked, I held my babies close, and for the first time in what felt like forever, I saw myself from the outside – a mother doing her best. There were dark circles under my eyes, yes, but also love in every line of my face, strength in every quiet touch.

My mom stood off to the side, watching with teary eyes and a proud smile. She knew what this meant. That day wasn't just about the pictures – it was about being seen, loved, and reminded of the beauty in the middle of the mess. It was a gift I didn't know I needed, and one I'll never forget.

Abuse and My Birthday

As the weeks wore on, the emotional toll of my husband's abuse deepened. What started as harsh words and criticism grew into a constant stream of verbal attacks: belittling me, mocking my exhaustion, and dismissing my every plea for help with the babies.

I felt smaller by the day, like I was vanishing in plain sight. The few moments I once looked forward to, like my birthday, began to feel meaningless in the shadow of his anger and instability. I dreaded the idea of spending the day with him – pretending things were fine, faking smiles, and waiting for the next outburst.

Instead of suffering through the charade, I quietly reached out to my neighbor, Christina, a kind, grounded woman who hosted a baby shower with some of my friends.

"Hey, Christina, how are you?" I asked.

"Hey, Adele, doing well. Just getting off work. What's up?" Christina responded.

"Any chance you could come out to dinner with me later tonight? It's my birthday, and I want to enjoy it with someone fun and caring. Can you join us?" I pleaded.

"Well, Mike is out of town," she mentioned.

"Please, Christina. I need you to come," I asked insistently.

I told her the truth: I didn't feel safe or celebrated in my own home anymore. "Oh…okay. I can drive. I would love to celebrate with you," she understood.

Without hesitation, she came with us to dinner at The Melting Pot in downtown Littleton.

A Concern Arises

After returning from a wonderful dinner with Christina and my abusive husband, I took over the responsibilities from my mom as soon as we came home.

At about 10:30 p.m., I was getting Kingston and noticed he needed a diaper change. Something startled me when I opened his diaper: "Oh my gosh, what is this? I mean, I know he is a boy and he has testicles, but what are these two egg-shaped hard things above his genitals? Oh my gosh, his belly button is extended and totally sticking out."

I immediately texted pictures to our family doctor, who had given me her cell phone number. She scheduled Kingston to be seen the next day.

Upon arrival, she mentioned he may have three hernias in his lower abdominal cavity and she gave me a referral to consult with a doctor where the triplets stayed for neonatal care.

In the afternoon on December 22, we met Dr. Campana, who explained that Kingston had three hernias: two in his abdominal cavity and one in his umbilical. My son Kingston was scheduled to have surgery the following day at 3:30 p.m. in the afternoon.

I was consumed by so much anxiety. My sweet baby is just two months old – so fragile, so small – and the idea of him being put under anesthesia and undergoing surgery felt unbearable. I packed an overnight bag carefully, folding a few things I needed with trembling hands, preparing for an overnight stay, hoping that Kingston would be well enough so we could all spend our first Christmas together.

Because he was a preemie, staying in the PICU wasn't a choice, but mandatory after the hernia repair. I braced myself to be strong for him, to hold it together in that sterile hospital room, while my heart was pounding at every beep of the monitor.

What I wasn't prepared for was the shock of what came next.

Waves of Betrayal

When I mentioned to Akuma I had already planned to stay with our son post-op, he told me, "No, I am going to stay with him."

We argued for some time about it, and I figured, you know what, let's just flip a coin. I chose tails; if I get tails I stay, if not, I'll go home.

We flipped the coin; it landed on heads.

The fact that my husband argued with me, knowing full well that I planned and packed a bag to care for my son while he needed to stay overnight or more days in the hospital, blew my mind. The fact that he wanted to stay and care for our son, but he didn't want to do the same for me – something in me broke that night. He had never shown me that kind of willingness when it was me in the hospital – when I was barely clinging to life after delivering our triplets. Back just a few months ago, he didn't stay. He didn't show up in the ways I desperately needed.

I went through that trauma alone, recovering from major surgery and complications, fighting infections, and trying to be a mother from a wheelchair – while he came and went as he pleased, but now, suddenly he was stepping in.

For the baby.

Not for me.

The betrayal hit me like a wave, not because I didn't want him to care for our son, but because it laid bare how little care he had shown for me. It reminded me that when I was at my weakest, he hadn't seen me as someone worth standing by.

Once Kingston was out of surgery and back in the PICU room, I sat with him for a few hours, watching his tiny chest rise and fall under the tubes and wires – feeling not only fear for him, but a raw, aching grief for the support I never got.

I gathered my overnight bag and went home to care for Reece and Scarlett. Thoughts ran through my head on my way home, crying and hating the situation all at once. I processed it in pieces, not all at the same time. At first, I tried to take it at face value – that maybe, just maybe, Akuma was stepping up to care for our son in the PICU, while I took care of our other two children. A rare moment of responsibility.

But as the hours passed into the midnight wakings and feedings, the pieces quickly fell into place – a cold realization settled in. Akuma wasn't staying out of love or concern. He wasn't suddenly overcome with fatherly devotion. He was staying because someone else – trained hospital staff – would be caring for our son. He knew the nurses would be monitoring vitals, giving meds, feeding, changing, and watching every detail, and with that, he saw his way out. He saw a parenting break. A nearly quiet room. A place to rest. A night of uninterrupted sleep he hadn't earned.

It dawned on me earlier while I was hauling a bag through the hospital corridors, comforting our son before surgery, holding his tiny hand while mine trembled with fear. I was on edge, never sitting still, mind racing with every "what if." I was parenting in the trenches – again – while he took refuge under the guise of sacrifice. That realization crushed me. He didn't do it to help. It was an escape. It was for convenience. More than anything, it reminded me – painfully – that when it truly mattered, when I was the one who needed rest, compassion, and care, he never chose me.

Kingston's surgery went well. There were no obstacles or loops to go through, and on Christmas Eve, Kingston was sent home just in time to celebrate Christmas as a family.

Our First Christmas

Christmas morning was busy and exhausting; it had become my new normal. We were all downstairs sitting on the couch, my mom, the babies and I enjoying Christmas morning together, when suddenly, Akuma walked in wearing one of my favorite maternity shirts.

"Oh, I see you are wearing my favorite shirt," I laughed.

He walked behind my mom so she couldn't see the middle finger he held in front to show me he didn't care for my comment.

The holidays used to hold so much promise. I had always imagined our first Thanksgiving and Christmas as a family – soft lights glowing, babies bundled in cozy pajamas, laughter filling the house. But instead, those days became some of the most painful reminders of what was missing, of what was broken.

There were no shared moments of gratitude, no warmth at the table. Just tension, cold shoulders, and the ever-growing weight of being invisible in my own home. Christmas morning should have been magical. I had dreamed it would be. It was the gift I wanted to unwrap, but it never came true.

New Year, New Challenges

As the new year arrived, I held onto a fragile hope that things could still get better – that somehow, with enough effort, love, and determination, we could turn the page. Not much had changed. The tension was still there; the coldness between us grew thicker and unspoken. The exhaustion of raising our triplets, with just a few helpers from my mom and my sister, was challenging emotionally and physically, and it still pressed down on me daily.

I began having physical difficulties postpartum in my feet and in my spine where the spinal block was injected. I had gone to see a specialist at the end of December right around the triplets' two-month wellness check to get my feet looked at.

I had developed severe plantar fasciitis in both of my feet, probably from the weight I carried from my pregnancy with multiples and from not recovering as my doctor instructed by avoiding strenuous tasks. I was often left to carry the bucket seats alone, and Akuma was never supportive of my recovery.

The pain was pretty severe; I had pain throughout the day from the moment of waking to the moment of lying down for interrupted sleep. I was given custom shoe inserts, but the pain never subsided. Walking into the nursery was painful every time, and sometimes I would have to crawl around to get to my babies to care for them and tend to their needs.

I also had pain where my spinal block was injected; it made it difficult to stand for more than thirty minutes at any given time, and it also made sitting down for roughly the same amount of time, just as painful. Filling formula bottles for an hour had to be done in increments of time, so I could bend over or rest before finishing.

I continually told myself that maybe he was overwhelmed, just like I was. Maybe he didn't know how to show up, but with time and patience, he could learn. So, I softened my voice, bit my tongue, and made space for peace even when I was the one hurting. I poured out even more energy into our home, into the children, and into trying to hold it all together. I read marriage books, suggested counseling, proposed date nights, and convinced myself that love meant pushing through the pain.

I was determined – determined to fight for something that once held promise, determined not to let go too easily, determined to protect my children from a broken home – no matter how broken I already felt inside. Even in my own resolve, there was a quiet knowing – trying to make a marriage work when you're the only one trying is its own kind of heartbreak.

The Support of Many

I moved into gear, and so did my sister and mom. Once the triplets had reached their three-month mark, we started organizing extra help. We all chose people we trusted deeply to pitch in: our hairdresser, college friends, IVF friends, Bible study friends, neighbors, friends of trusted friends, our church, a ministry called Love in Action, triplet mom friends, teacher friends, the Mormon church – even though we didn't share the same beliefs, they loved babies. We posted church bulletins for volunteer help; you name it, we did it.

Suddenly, people were signing up on a volunteer calendar I had on my kitchen counter. I had morning shift helpers, midday helpers, early evening helpers and bedtime helpers. Help was coming in singles, married couples, families, helpers coming in pairs and in threes – I was able to rest, recover more, and do formula runs.

We had a meal train set up for food delivery, so I didn't have to remain on my "Three C" diet of dried cereal, chocolate and coffee – on repeat. I hadn't used silverware in months, so the thought of having real food and being able to enjoy it sounded amazing.

Early in the year, I was gifted by my grandmother Ya Ya and my mom a night nanny. She helped randomly on "once in a blue moon" nights to tend to the triplets, so Akuma and I could get a full eight hours of sleep. She was remarkable and somehow magically did things for my babies that I couldn't figure out – she kept them quiet all night long during the feedings, did laundry, folded it and put things away all before sunrise.

The Love Language of Physical Touch

Since I had extra help, I had time for myself, and I would take the opportunity to get massages to soothe my achy feet and rejuvenate my soul. I tried as often as I could to get two-hour massages – one hour on my feet and the other on the rest of my body. When that wasn't an option, I opted for quick massages at Whole Foods market.

One of the hardest things to admit, even to myself, was how deeply I craved connection. Physical touch has always been my love language. A gentle hand on my back, a quiet hug at the end of a hard day, even small gestures like brushing past each other in the kitchen with warmth – it all made me feel seen, safe, and valued. However, somewhere along the way, intimacy vanished. Four months had passed since the birth of our children, and I could only recall one time when he chose to make love to me.

My husband stopped touching me. There were no more kisses goodnight, no arms wrapping around me in the quiet moments. The space between us in bed grew wider and colder. He often broke the intimacy of sleeping in the same bed and instead would sleep on the couch in our living room.

Initially, I told myself it was the stress, the exhaustion of parenting newborns, but as the weeks turned to months, I realized it wasn't temporary – it was deliberate. He had withdrawn, not just emotionally, but physically, leaving me aching in a silence that cut deeper than any argument.

Consequently, when he distanced himself from me, I no longer asked. I found myself getting massages, not only to help the agonizing reality of the bilateral plantar fasciitis but because I missed being touched. To feel the masseuse's hands on my back and my feet, even knowing it wasn't for affection or out of a desire to touch me; it was a simple act of the physical connection I craved. I could ask for a massage and not be rejected. Those moments, brief as they were, became my only lifeline to closeness. I would close my eyes and pretend it meant more than it did, because the alternative – the man I married no longer wanted to touch me at all – was too painful to sit with.

And still – I stayed. Still, I hoped. But every day and night, every step he took away from me, felt like a quiet confirmation of what I feared most: that I was no longer loved the way I needed to be, and maybe…no longer loved at all.

Valentine's Day

Valentine's Day was a few days away, and I wanted to make Akuma feel loved. I had some helpers the day I decided to make Akuma all these homemade "Love Coupons" to encourage love and a desire to connect with, not necessarily intimately, but a connection of some sort.

I made date night coupons, massage coupons, watch a movie coupons, make dinner together coupons, game night coupons, do a Bible devotion together coupons, and lots of hang out with the guys coupons. I worked for hours handwriting these coupons hoping he would love that I took the time to do all of this for him.

I knew our nights out, let alone our days out were not frequent since the triplets were still in the, "It's cold and flu season – do not go out except for wellness visits or for a brief walk close to home" phase. So, I knew this would mean a lot to him.

The joy I desired was short-lived.

Over the next several weeks, the only coupons he gave me were the ones I had made a plethora of – hang out with the guys nights. It was clearly evident – he wanted nothing to do with me.

March was quickly approaching, and the triplets' five-month mark was around the corner. Our sixth wedding anniversary was as well. The exhaustion of everything was beginning to lessen in some ways. Scarlett began sleeping through the night and was sleeping at least ten hours. I had to believe it was her Valentine's Day gift to me. I had developed really good routines with my children. I knew what to expect at every feeding and how many ounces of formula would be drunk. I had a schedule of playtime, naptime, and bedtime routines all in the mix.

Hidden From the Light

We were almost done with the recommendations from the NICU of reducing light – where for months we had only one stimulus displayed, our Christmas tree lights. They were our guiding light since we had set it up on November 6th when Reece was getting ready to come home from the NICU.

Our Christmas tree was still up, and it was finally coming down in March. The blinds in our house were always drawn closed – solely for our babies. The NICU doctors and staff had explained how calm, dim environments helped preemies conserve calories; how too much stimulation could overwhelm their tiny systems. So, I kept the lights low, the house quiet, the blinds shut tight. It was for their health. It made so much sense. However, over time, those drawn blinds became more than just a medical recommendation – they became a reflection of how I felt inside.

Hidden.

Shut off.

Alone.

While the world outside moved on with its seasons and celebrations, I sat in a darkened room, feeding, burping, changing, surviving – on repeat. The walls started to close in. The silence wasn't peaceful; it was heavy. The blinds shielded us from the sun, yes, but they also shielded the truth I didn't want anyone to see – that inside my house I was drowning.

Even though I had an army set up to help – only my sister, my mom, and my closest friends knew what was going on behind closed doors and the very depths of my heart. The days blurred together in dim light as the daily tasks of tending to the preemies and my own postpartum health issues with my feet and my back.

Akuma returned to work after he took two months off to help me care for the preemies after delivery. I did gain some "light" back when others came to help, yet my nights were filled with the quiet ache of loneliness. I never felt so invisible, so removed from the life I used to know.

The blinds stayed closed and so did I.

That's why it was surprising to me when Akuma desired to take me out for our sixth-year anniversary.

"Del, I won a dinner at this restaurant downtown, Vesta Dipping Grill. I was thinking I could take you there for our anniversary," he kindly suggested.

"Wow! Really? Out to dinner? A break from doing what I do all day and night? I'll gladly take it!" I announced.

"Great, I'll make the reservation. Let's plan for our anniversary night on Friday," Akuma suggested.

"Perfect! We have a few more nights available with our night nanny we can use. I'll call to see if she is available," I happily thought.

We had organized our, "once in a blue moon" night nanny to take over so we could enjoy a night out without a care in the world and to come home to get a full night of sleep. The night would be perfect.

Our 6th Wedding Anniversary

The night before our anniversary, there were a lot of hiccups in the midnight feedings. We were both so exhausted. I nudged Akuma to get up for the next feeding.

"Ugh…already…ugh…I'm so tired," I thought to myself. I nudged Akuma with my arm to get up.

"Akuma, it's your turn to get Scarlett," I sleepily said.

"No, it's your turn!" he snapped.

"No, it's *your* turn!" I snapped back, "Go, Scarlett is screaming."

Moments of silence...

"*Go, Akuma,* go get Scarlett for her feeding," I stressed.

"*Dammit.* Fine," he scoffed.

The morning of our anniversary, I felt groggy, yet I wanted today to be special because, for once in five long and lonely months, Akuma wanted to connect with me.

"Good morning, Akuma. Happy Anniversary!" I beamed.

Silence.

No response.

Not even a hello...good morning... nothing.

As Akuma was getting ready for work by taking his shower, I was doing my morning routine. I had Kingston in the swing, and without hesitation, I began to weep.

I stared at Kingston, and he stared right back at me as if he knew everything I felt in that moment. It wasn't a slow, quiet cry – it was the cry. The kind that comes from somewhere buried so deep it feels ancient. I had been carrying so much for so long – recovering from the trauma of birth that nearly took my life, waking through endless nights to care for three fragile preemies, pouring every ounce of myself into trying to hold together a crumbling marriage. Smiling when I needed to cry. Giving, when I had nothing left.

I wept. Not soft tears – but shaking, breathless sobs that racked through my body. I sat in the recliner, wrapped my arms around myself because no one else could. No one was there to embrace me at this moment.

I cried for the woman I used to be. For the mother I was trying so hard to become. For the wife who kept hoping for love that never returned. I cried for the nights I held babies while silently screaming inside. For the days I tried to keep the house quiet, the lights low, the pain hidden. I cried for the invisibility, the inadequacy, the crushing sense that no matter how much I did, it would never be enough for him. That I was never enough.

It was the kind of cry that emptied me.

When it was over, I sat there quietly and prayed. I knew something had changed. I couldn't un-feel it. I couldn't un-know how deeply broken I had become just trying to survive.

"Lord, Jesus, I am at my wit's end here. Either this marriage is going to work, and you are going to show me how to make it work, or it's not. And if it's not, can you please show me signs? Because I cannot continue to tolerate this abuse and horrible behavior of Akuma. I have tried. I have no idea what is wrong with him. He is detached and rude. He is an eyesore to be around. I cannot do this anymore. Please help, Jesus. Amen."

That night we went to Vesta Dipping Grill for a meal. The conversation was vague and somewhat appalling to my senses.

"So, we finally get some alone time," Akuma giggled with sarcasm.

"Yeah, it's nice to have a break from it all," I acknowledged.

"So, I was thinking, wouldn't it be cool to renew our vows?" he suggested surprisingly.

The thoughts in my head swirled in disgust.

Now? Why the heck would you want to renew our vows? You have done nothing to even suggest that would be an option. After months of emotional abuse – of being dismissed, belittled, neglected, and made to feel like a burden instead of a partner – the suggestion of renewing our vows felt like a cruel twist of irony. It didn't bring hope or excitement. It brought confusion. Numbness. Even rage, buried under layers of exhaustion.

How could he speak of vows when he had broken every one that mattered? When he turned his back on me in my most vulnerable moments? When his words had torn through my self-worth, leaving me to question my sanity, my value, my strength.

There was something hollow in his proposal – like he wanted the image of love without the substance. A performance of commitment, not the real thing. He hadn't apologized. He hadn't changed. He hadn't seen me…and now he wanted a ceremony?

The idea of standing across from him again, promising loyalty, love and partnership felt like a betrayal to myself. Like I'd be validating all the harm he caused. Like I'd be silencing the voice inside me that had spent months screaming, "**This is not what I deserve. This is not what the triplets deserve.**"

Instead of romance, his suggestion felt like gaslighting. Like he was rewriting the story to erase the pain he caused, painting himself as a husband worthy of vows – when I was still stitching together the parts of me, he broke.

It didn't feel like a new beginning.

It felt like a lie.

"Renew our vows? You act like you don't even want to be married…" I reprimanded.

* * * * * *

At the beginning of March, Akuma mentioned he wanted to work on his resume. He told me he desired to make it more presentable to show the work he had successfully done at his current prestigious employer and to seek new employment, to gain better pay to care for the triplets and me.

Since I received my degree at the university and had the ability to write well, I told Akuma I would be happy to help him with this task. His resume went from okay to outstanding with my help.

Akuma was bilingual; he was fluent in English and Spanish. He was also able to speak a little bit of Italian and Portuguese. He was a well-rounded individual whom I thought could work anywhere being multi-lingual.

* * * * * *

Hidden in Plain Sight

The day after our dinner at Vesta Dipping Grill was Saturday. Akuma told me he had to work that day.

"Hey Adele, I am going to get ready for work. I need to take a shower. Oh, and remember Cole, Jack, and Dana you met a while back on Aster's birthday? Well, Cole invited me over to hang out with him after work today. He invited a bunch of our co-workers to hang out at his apartment," Akuma informed me.

"Oh, yeah, Cole. He was so great. That's kind of him. Okay, will you be back for the bedtime routine with the triplets?" I asked as I was getting one of the boys ready for tummy time.

"No, we're going to hang out at his apartment and relax in the hot tub," he responded.

"Oh, that sounds relaxing," I whispered to myself, "hey, do you mind if I use the restroom before you take your shower?" I asked expectantly.

"Sure, that's fine, just hurry up. I have to eat a quick breakfast and get on the road so I can beat the morning traffic," he asserted.

"Oh, I'll make it quick," I replied.

I entered the bathroom and locked the door behind me to sit down and use the toilet. I immediately noticed Akuma's phone unlocked on the bathroom counter. I thought to myself, "Wow, he left his phone in here. He never lets me look at his phone." The screen was still lit up and it was *unlocked* – a rare window into the world he always kept guarded. My heart jumped into my throat. I wasn't someone who went through phones. I didn't want to be *that* person, but, after months of feeling invisible, unloved, and discarded, I had to know if the way he was treating me had another explanation – if there was someone, or something else besides the male postpartum depression I excused his toxic behavior with to friends and family for months after the delivery.

My fingers trembled. "Do I do it? No… it's not polite, but what if this is how God wants to tell me if this marriage should work or not?" Okay…just for a little bit.

"I'm going number two…I promise to make it quick. Sorry, it must've been the early morning coffee," I lied aloud, but I had to know.

I picked up the phone. I quickly looked at his Facebook. No, nothing there. I pulled up his pictures, scrolled a bit. Ugh…ugh…no, nothing. Then, I opened up his email account. Most of it was mundane – promotions, spam, a few unread work messages. But then, one subject line caught my eye – "Dennis1806, There Are New Singles in Your Area!" It wasn't explicit. Just interesting… I paused.

Put the phone down.

"Who the heck is Dennis?"

I panicked and thought, "Is this something to focus on?

New singles in your area?

Oh. You. Bet."

I noticed the email had already been opened, so I clicked on it to see who the email was from. It was a website I didn't recognize. What the heck was that? I stared at it, frozen. My chest tightened. I wasn't sure if I was seeing it right. I told myself not to overreact, but to just remember a few things when I left the bathroom. I kept saying this in my mind as if it were a broken record – Dennis1806…Dennis1806… Dennis1806…Dennis1806…1806…1806…I locked it in my memory. I placed his phone exactly as he had it and locked his phone before I flushed the toilet and walked out.

"Hey Akuma, I'm done. Thanks so much for letting me go potty," I was more thankful than he knew.

Something was going to unravel; I could feel it under my skin. The truth needed to be found and I thought to myself conspicuously – I knew this man was up to no good.

Akuma had showered and was about ready to leave for work. I noticed this brown paper grocery bag with his after-work items for his outing with Cole and his co-workers. He had his swim trunks, a few other personal belongings, and what I found to be odd – a toothbrush and toothpaste.

What "guy" get together involves you packing your own toothbrush and toothpaste? None that I know of. I mean, I could think of fresh mint chewing gum or Tic-Tacs, but not a toothbrush and toothpaste. It had B.S. written all over it.

"Bye, have a great day at work," I smiled and watched him walk to the car, hop in, and drive away.

Web of Lies

I knew right away I wanted to find out who Dennis1806 was.

I sat down on the couch while the triplets were in their bouncers and swings, while I pulled up this website I knew nothing about. I finally had that moment to slow down and do the research.

It was 7:56 a.m. when I discovered what it was. I typed out the words into the search bar. I wasn't sure what I expected to find – maybe a dating website, maybe something sketchy, but harmless. As the page loaded, the truth hit me like I had been run over by a train.

"Life is short. Have an affair."

That's their slogan. Their entire mission.

My stomach turned. My hands went cold. It wasn't subtle. He wasn't even trying to pretend to be innocent. This was a discreet dating website built for betrayal – for people who were married, partnered, supposedly committed – to seek secret affairs, and Akuma had been there. He had engaged with this, somehow. He was Dennis1806. Behind my back. All while I was breaking my body and soul to hold our family together.

It was like watching the final puzzle piece fall into place – but instead of relief, I felt sick. Disgusted. A visceral, burning shame that wasn't mine to carry, but still wrapped around me like poison. I thought of the sleepless nights I spent bottle feeding our babies, the tears I cried alone in the dark, the desperate attempts I made to fix a marriage I didn't even know was being sabotaged.

He was planning to be unfaithful or maybe he already was.

He did it while I was bleeding, broken, and trying to survive.

I stared at the slogan – "Life is short. Have an affair." Something inside me shattered because I realized in that moment: he already had. Maybe not physically. Maybe not yet. But emotionally and spiritually – he had stepped out. Left me in the dust. No vow renewal, no empty apology, no performance of love would ever undo what I knew now. I had to know more. I studied this shady website and tried looking up his profile – "Dennis1806".

However, my motherly duties were calling. It was a mix of researching different ways to find Dennis1806 and an all-consuming blend of love, exhaustion, and logistics.

The pace was nonstop.

The babies had a more predictable eating and sleeping schedule now, yet with three in the mix, there's never a true break. It's a rotation of needs, a rhythm only a mother could understand. There were usually a mix of simultaneous or staggered cries coming from the nursery. I moved from crib to crib, lifting sleepy little bodies, changing diapers, and preparing bottle number four since midnight. Feeding took time; sometimes I could feed two at once, sometimes I had to get creative.

Mothers of multiples were experts at this. Multiple mouths to soothe, burp, and clean, and hold close. By the time the last baby finished, the first one needed a new outfit, and another had spit up from acid reflux all over themselves.

Next came more tummy time for the other two, an essential activity for building neck strength and motor skills. Of course, I needed to take pictures of them because they look absolutely adorable.

After pictures, I grabbed my phone again to look for Dennis1806.

Of course, I had to pause because I forgot to eat with all these new developments since 6:45 a.m. this morning.

Back to looking, and I cannot locate Dennis1806. I attempted another approach. I typed in his age: 50, no match.

Then I thought, "Wait, if he could lie to me all this time, he would definitely lie about his age." I typed in 40 to 45. Nothing.

Back to the grind, Reece woke up and was fussy – soiled diaper. I turned up the white noise machine and made sure the curtains were blacked out. Fresh pampers and he fell right back to sleep. I crawled out of the room and slithered low to the floor to leave without the other two seeing me.

I typed in black and Latino. Nothing yet.

By late afternoon, I had the colorful play mat set up for Scarlett to look up and play with. I had Kingston set up in the swing and Reece in a bouncer. I was warming up bottle number…bottle number…I've lost count.

Finally, at about 4:29 p.m., I recalled what I helped Akuma do about a month earlier – his resume. I typed in – fluent in Spanish, English, Italian, and Portuguese – I said a little prayer – and – *Voila!* There he was.

Dennis1806 is attached…*wow…well at least he mentions he is married. Wow, he has aged backwards, younger than me? Well, you don't say, Dennis, thirty-four years young.* His slogan: "The Best Is Yet to Come". *Is it now? Okay, his height, yep, he wrote his correct height. I mean, you cannot really lie about that when someone sees you in person. Weight – 155. He is pretty skinny and scrawny.* Body type – muscular – *bwahahahaaaaa – such a lie. Oh, interesting a topic titled* Limits – Whatever Excites Me. *Wow…no words.* Ethnicity – other. *No wonder I couldn't find him.* Languages – English, Portuguese (Brasil), Italian, Spanish – *BINGO!*

Okay, let's see what else… Interests with a fill in the blank

*I'm **open to*** - Looking for a nice woman to have some intimate discreet encounters with! Nothing life-changing and nothing complicated – just some NSA! W*hat the heck is NSA? Let me look that one up…No Strings Attached…*

okay what else...just some NSA! I'm a very nice, polite guy I would love a woman who is in the same situation as me, married doesnt bug me *(you forgot an apostrophe)*, as I dont judge, *(missed another apostrophe)* nor want to be judged!

Wow...pathetic. Okay, what else.

My turn-Ons – someone that hates drama and love to have fun . *(His grammar is awful)*

I'm looking for – I'm so romantic to make myself and a woman enjoy every minute of our time.

I read everything in about two minutes.

I need to find out what he is doing behind my back.

I have a certain feeling he is not going to hang out with Cole tonight, especially knowing he brought his own toothpaste and toothbrush. Seriously? Who does that? What guy does this?

I need to know what he is doing. I want to find out, but how? I needed to make a plan.

Evening came, brought on with the bedtime routine I had established around the three-month mark – cute cozy footed jammies, lotion, new pampers off to the side, along with everything I needed for bedtime.

I discovered the only parts newborns and my five-month-old babies were dirty – were their butts and their faces. So, I set aside a warm soapy tub with washcloths, used as "dirty" for their bottoms, and a warm "clean" water tub with clean washcloths for their faces.

Once I had finished "Butt and Faces", it was a full-body massage, songs, a bedtime story, and finally cozy jammies for bed. Followed by our favorite lullaby, and it was goodnight for Scarlett and a few hours of sleep for the boys.

At first, I realized those nights I spent in quiet defeat – curled up on the edge of the bed, wondering if maybe he was struggling, too. Maybe it was male postpartum depression. Maybe the coldness, the distance, the absence of love and support wasn't cruelty – it was pain.

I always gave him the benefit of the doubt over and over, softening my own needs to make room for what I thought might be his silent suffering. I wasn't just heartbroken – I was earnestly worried for him.

But then, something in me shifted today.

It wasn't rage that took over. It was profound clarity.

It was like a switch flipped off in my brain – subtle, but undeniable. One moment, I was the invisible, exhausted wife trying to hold everything together…the next, I became someone else. Not angry. Not hysterical. But alert. Focused. Observant.

I recollected TV shows I used to watch – The First 48, Law and Order – and how investigators didn't rely on emotion; they gathered facts. They looked past the performance. They tracked the inconsistencies, followed timelines, and noticed patterns.

I started to realize I didn't need to explain away his behavior anymore. I needed to observe it. I stopped pleading. I started paying attention.

Where was he really going tonight? Why was he always sleeping on the couch? What times did he leave and return? What energy did he save for the outside world that I never saw at home? I began logging it all in the back of my mind, calmly and quietly, like I was building a case – not to accuse yet, but to understand.

Something definitely was off.

For once, I wasn't going to be the one crying in the dark, blaming myself. I had spent enough time feeling invisible. Now I had a part to play – and this time, it wasn't the victim.

I was the woman who had stopped waiting for the truth to come to her.

I was going to find the truth out for myself, and with that, I came up with a brilliant plan, hoping I would be able to stack the deck and let the cards fall as they may. Would I be able to pull it off? Time would tell.

Akuma came home around 9:30 p.m. later that night. I was already in bed when he walked in.

"Hey Akuma, how was work? How was your time with Cole and your friends?" I questioned in a sleepy tone.

"It was great. We were in the hot tub most of the time," he told me.

"I'm sure you were. Hot tubbing all evening...you and your toothbrush and toothpaste," I thought to myself. I turned on my left side, turned out the light, and fell sound asleep.

An Unremarkable Series of Events

On Sunday, Akuma was getting ready for work once more. He got dressed in his three-piece suit and was out the door for his shift.

Today was a very special outing. Today was Marie's sister's bridal shower at a local hangout close to downtown Denver.

We were at the end of our "cold and flu" season for the triplets, who had only been having outings for wellness visits and short walks close to home, so I wanted to make this a very special occasion. It was not only to celebrate Gwen, but to celebrate my very first girlie outing with my daughter, Scarlett. I was thrilled to dress her up and have an official opportunity to show her off. She was beautiful from the moment I laid eyes on her the day after delivery. I had help lined up for Kingston and Reece to stay home with someone to look after them and found myself on cloud nine.

I also had a few other things up my sleeve for my plan. However, I needed to move quickly before the bridal brunch started at 12:30 p.m. sharp that afternoon.

I needed to find a picture on my phone to use, but which one? It couldn't be a picture of me. It had to be a cover. I had roughly three hours to put this together, but how?

Finally, I figured it out.

My sweet friend Faith recently had her sister do my hair at my own house because getting out wasn't an option.

"Yes, that picture I took of that girl online that I wanted my cut like…yes, so perfect. Let me pull it up," I thought.

I moseyed back over to the discreet dating site and set up an account. I needed a username, but which one? Something that would catch his eye…something catchy, something cheap. Yes! I giggled and laughed aloud…SugarNSpicy is so perfect.

Can I pull this off? This is such good detective work.

Okay, I need to share who I am. The thought, "New singles in your area!" popped into my mind. Ha, yes! I am going to say I am single and young, age twenty-three, fresh out of college. Yes! He loved Boulder and always has. I am going to say I graduated from CU Boulder. What else would he like to hear or see? Okay, let's see…oh, my slogan. "Hola Guapo's!" to show that I speak Spanish. He would like that. He would probably like me to be shorter, so 5'4. I'm gonna run with that for now. I can fill out the rest later. Oh wait, let me favorite him since it's an option for now. Maybe a quick message…. hmmm…something that shows I read his profile.

The waiting game began…

The bridal shower was the perfect mix of laughter, lighthearted games, and girlie conversations that filled the room with warmth and excitement. The space was decorated in soft spring colors – blush pinks, creams, greens and a touch of gold – with delicate floral arrangements on every table and a mimosa bar sparkling in the corner. The air smelled faintly of fresh roses and vanilla cupcakes, and Gwen glowed with anticipation.

Guests arrived in colorful dresses and soft curls, greeting each other with hugs and chatter. The energy was warm and familiar, like a reunion of women who were happy to celebrate love and all the little details that go with it.

The games kicked off with a few classics – "How well do you know the bride?" had everyone laughing at quirky answers and sweet memories. Then came the toilet paper wedding dress contest, where teams wrapped each other in layers of tissue, turning the room into a runway of giggles and creativity.

Between games, there were dainty finger foods – cucumber sandwiches, mini quiches, fruit skewers, and sparkly macarons in shades that matched the décor.

Gwen looked gorgeous and was elated. We were all just oozing with excitement for her upcoming wedding. It was the kind of afternoon where time slowed down just enough to savor the sweetness. A room full of women, celebrating not just the bride's future, but the sisterhood that lifted her up along the way.

It was also a time to celebrate with my sweet daughter, Scarlett. Everyone who came to celebrate with Gwen also had the chance to meet Scarlett for the very first time. It was a moment suspended in joy – a soft, glowing pause after months of waiting, praying and hoping to hold her close. It wasn't just an introduction – it was a homecoming, a gathering of love that had been building from afar since the day she was born.

"She looks just like you," someone said.

"Awe, she is so beautiful, Adele," Gwen glowed.

The room buzzed with soft laughter, the clinking of glasses, and the hum of life beginning. Stories were shared, hugs exchanged, and every person there became part of her story – her first time being celebrated by many I cared about.

We saw sunshine that day. It was beautiful. Unforgettable. A first meeting wrapped up in grace.

Bzzzt!...my phone must've received a message. Let me see. No text messages. Let me look at my email. Oh. My. Gosh. OMG! Whaaat!!!

I had opened my fake profile. One message waiting...

Dennis1806 – Hi SugarNSpicy love to meet you. Here is my cell number...*Oh my goodness, you are giving her, I mean me, I mean her your real phone number! What a*...**I'm off today let me know. I just finish working out shoot me a text or call**. *What a sec...if Akuma isn't at work, where the heck is he?*

We had been celebrating Gwen for quite some time. We got there shortly after noon and now it was roughly 3:26 in the afternoon.

I had to excuse myself from this celebration to continue to plan my cover and incredible detective work.

I decided I would write Dennis1806 back. I had to know what he was doing. I wasn't expecting to hear from Dennis1806 so quickly, yet within twenty-two minutes he had already written SugarNSpicy back.

At first there was disbelief. The signs were there, the confirmation of what I just read felt surreal. It was like my world tilted off axis – everything I thought I knew was now very questionable.

Marriage should be built on trust, and when it's broken, it cuts deeper than almost anything else. My heart had been stabbed over and over, month after month – not because of the act, but because someone I vowed to love through it all with my whole heart chose to be so deceitful and it felt that my worth was ignored entirely.

Anger was a natural response – not only at him, but I was angry at myself for being so blind. How did I not know this until now? If this is just one instance, there could be plenty more.

I sat there frozen in place, my eyes wide and darting, as if searching for an exit that didn't exist. My chest rose and fell rapidly. I had to hand over Scarlett to my mom and I walked upstairs from the celebration to gather my thoughts. My breath became shallow and faint, like I couldn't get enough air no matter how hard I tried.

One hand clutched my chest, the other my phone, and my hands trembled uncontrollably. A wave of heat flushed over my skin, followed by a sudden chill that made me break into a sweat. My heart thumped violently in my chest, so loud and fast, it felt like it might burst. I doubled over slightly, pressing my palm to my sternum as I was trying to calm the storm inside me.

My thoughts spiraled. I couldn't breathe. The room blurred around me. It was as if my hearing was muffled like it was underwater. A heavy fog settled into my mind.

"Del, are you okay? What is going on?" my mom panicked.

"Mom, I think I'm having a panic attack. I discovered something this morning, well…yesterday…" I tapered off.

I gave her a brief synopsis of what I discovered and what I was up to.

At this time, a family friend came up and wanted to know what happened to me. She brought me a glass of ice water to help me calm down.

"I want to meet him and call him out on his infidelity. That…" I was enraged.

"No, let's not do anything yet. Let's think logically," our family friend offered, "what do you want the outcome to look like? Do you want to file for divorce?"

"Yes, I am not going to stay married to him! He is pathetic! A liar!" I bellowed.

"Okay, do you think you can play pretend, like, act you don't know anything for a little while longer, so we can help find someone to help us with serving him papers and file with the court, find a lawyer?" she disclosed.

"Yes, I can. I discovered it yesterday morning and played dumb all afternoon and last night. See, I created a fake profile on this website, and he took the bait. He actually took the bait!" I exclaimed.

"Wow, Adele…I'm impressed. You are already playing the part. Okay, respond to keep the dialogue going, but make an excuse…. something came up…something. I want you to keep him engaged. You can use this in court," we all agreed with what our friend had to say.

With the website covered, I decided to text Akuma as his wife and since he was "at work" just ten minutes away, I figured this would be a great time to bring Scarlett and be able to show her off to Akuma's co-workers. Many of his co-workers knew we had triplets.

So, I sent a text message to his phone, the same phone number he gave to SugarNSpicy.

Me: Hey Akuma, Scarlett and I are just finishing up with the bridal shower. We are just a few minutes away. I would love to show your co-workers our sweet baby girl.

Akuma: Sorry, now isn't a good time. I'm busy.

Me: Really? Even just for 5 – 10 minutes.

Akuma: Sorry, lots going on right now. We have line up and I need to go. Let's plan for next time.

Smooth, Akuma. Smooth. I know you aren't even there. So, where are you?

Akuma didn't get home Sunday night until well past ten o'clock in the evening. I did receive a couple of texts from him around 8:48 p.m.

Akuma: How are things? Leaving soon.

Will take over most of the night.

I had a feeling his guilt and shame was starting to sink in. I mean, after all, playing two people living a double life has to be exhausting, right? How do you remember the lies? How do you know what you said and what you didn't? It sounded pretty exhausting to me.

I took the time to respond to his text.
Me: Let's work as a team. 😊 The babies are all asleep.

I made small talk with the liar he is. We did our same night routine; they were growing and began to sleep a little more. It was still exhausting because sleep is a dream. It's a luxury I don't get often these days, yet I had to stay in the dark about what I knew.

Nothing You Pack for a Marriage

On Monday, Akuma was getting ready for another day of work. He had "worked" all weekend. Such dedication! I heard him in our bedroom rustling with something. I listened intently as I continued making my morning waffles in the toaster oven and heated up another cup of coffee. I heard some ripping, tearing of something…a few zips and a slam of the sliding bedroom closet door.

Abruptly, Akuma left the bedroom and walked to the bathroom to take his shower. I waited until I heard the shower turn on, the bath curtain slide open and then shut again.

I ran into the room and looked for the source of all the rustled noise – tears of paper, zips and bangs. I discovered a credit card receipt torn to shreds in the waste basket of all places. A gold mine. Inside the closet was that other bag Akuma took with him to work. I decided to figure out the trash later and looked inside his bag. I had to make it quick as I knew he usually took quick showers.

I unzipped the bag and found his deodorant spray I bought him months ago and the cologne I gave him on our sixth-year wedding anniversary. I found a vitamin bottle of something, and a petition to the United States to have his daughter from a previous marriage come live with us. Something heavy lay at the bottom of the bag. I pulled it out – Smucker's Boysenberry syrup – a brand-new bottle.

Interesting contents here. I remember he brought this bag with him the other day for his "Co-worker guy" get together. Swimsuits. Toothbrush. Toothpaste. Axe deodorant spray. Cologne. Boysenberry syrup. Of course – an infidelity kit.

I heard the shower curtain open and quickly grabbed the contents – gently placed everything in correct order, placed the bag zipped up on his side of the closet, and ran back to the kitchen to continue making breakfast.

Akuma walked out of the shower in his towel and walked back to our bedroom to get dressed. He had a habit of wearing these baggy cargo shorts under his work clothes which made no sense to me. No sense of style, let alone comfort, but he came out in his cargo shorts and a white T-shirt.

"Are you making waffles for breakfast?" Akuma asked.

"Oh, yeah. You want some?" I responded with another great idea.

"Yeah, that would be great," he said with gratitude.

I walked into the pantry to retrieve my favorite boysenberry syrup I had just bought the other day and to my surprise, it wasn't on the shelf.

I deliberately sounded extra loud and annoying when I announced aloud, "Akuma, I cannot find the boysenberry syrup I just bought at the store. I have looked on almost every shelf, and I cannot locate it?" I chose to sound unfashionably loud and confused. I stepped out of the pantry to sit down on the floor and do some tummy time with Kingston.

Out of the corner of my eye, I noticed Akuma walk from the kitchen into our bedroom. I heard him open the closet door, unzip the black bag, and out he sauntered holding the bottle of boysenberry syrup up his cargo pant leg with one hand clutching to the side of his pants back to the pantry.

I wanted to give him the chance to tell me the truth. Yet, what he did blew me away. Akuma and his sneaky ways, or so he thought.

"Here it is, it's right here. I found it! You must be going crazy!" he reported, making me sound like a lunatic.

"Oh, my goodness! Where was it?" I inquired.

"Just behind the cereal box, next to the flour," he informed me.

After we sat down and ate our waffles with the boysenberry syrup, Akuma was off to work, yet again.

I had some helpers from the mom of multiples group come help me with the triplets that morning. This meant I had more time to be a detective and go through the things I found in our bedroom earlier without having to stop so much to tend to the babies on my own. I had some laundry to take care of upstairs and one of the babies decided not to nap, so on various trips up and down the stairs I was able to get baby girl in the rocking bassinet and get all the laundry started.

My mom had a large island table in her open concept kitchen and living room, and I thought this would be the perfect time to dig out the trash contents and grab some Scotch tape to begin working on my paper puzzle.

In between laundry and tending to my baby girl, I was able to place everything in order. Several pages were ripped, and it took some time to assemble. I realized it was Akuma's credit card statement. The bill of $2,492.48 was due on April 20, 2015, with a minimum payment of $137.00 due.

First of all, we cannot afford to spend a bunch of money after just having the triplets five months ago. Second, I thought he was only using his credit card for emergencies, and lastly, I told him not to park downtown to go to work, but to take the light-rail to save money. Parking downtown is so expensive, especially now because baseball season is starting up and I know how $20 here and there can add up quickly.

Looks like he spent about $400 this past month…where…for what? Okay, let's look at his transactions.

February 24 – Phone Number XXX-XXX-XXXX CA	*$275.00*
February 23 – Central Parking	*$16.00*
February 24 – Hotel Stay	*$51.64*
February 27 – Central Parking	*$11.94*
March 5 – Whale Lot	*$10.00*
March 12 – Judo lot	*$20.00*
Late fee	*$35.00*

Well, he isn't paying his bills on time – that is not good. I see there are two big transactions on the same day. California and a hotel stay. Hmm…I know a couple of his uncles live in California. Did one of his uncles fly out and stay at a hotel? February…February…hmmm…doesn't ring a bell. That was right before the triplets were four months old.

Motherly duties called my name once more and I had to help get the triplets their morning bottles ready and dressed for the day. Afterwards, I called my mom and asked her to look up the phone number with the state of California attached to it. In the meantime, I was reading the triplets' books and singing to them while I ate my breakfast.

Soon after, I dug the black bag out of our closet and laid it down on the changing pad on the couch. I poured out all the contents and found the deodorant spray, the cologne I hated giving him for our anniversary, the paperwork to petition to send his daughter to live here, and what I thought were vitamins. I began to look through everything and had some thoughts pop up in my mind.

Since when would he have the time to write a petition? Where would she live? He cannot even take care of the triplets and me. We have lived in my mom's house since before the babies were born. He cannot even afford to get us a house, but he can do this – and do it behind my back? I will be taking this item and hiding it. What in the world?

Okay, onto the next item…okay, wait…this isn't a vitamin. Let's see here it says, "Support Blood Flow for Maximum Male Physical Performance: 75 Liquid Soft Gels". I dumped out its contents – there were eight left. Eight. This explains the couch sleeping. The hiding his phone. The late nights at "work". The lying. The distance. The "I cannot show up" to save my life. The lack of intimacy. We had sex once since the triplets had been born. Once. Where and who was he having sex with?

The answer to that question came soon enough.

"Adele, I have been texting and emailing you. Did you get my messages?" my mom urgently spoke.

"No, I've been looking at a few things, actually," I pointed out.

"That number you had me look up – it's an escort service. You know, like hiring someone for companionship. Maybe sexual favors, I'm not sure," my mom confirmed.

"Oh, I have to believe it was sexual," I maintained my stance, "Plus, he stayed at a hotel. It was definitely sexual. Eight Steel Red Libido pills left." I whispered to myself.

"Mom, I need to go," I quickly got off the phone.

I couldn't listen to this anymore. In three days' time, I had learned about a discreet website, Dennis1806, knew he wanted to engage in adulterous behavior, lied about being at work, lied about who he was on this website, found the boysenberry syrup, cologne, the eight pills, the petition – everything in our marriage was a lie. All of it.

Akuma didn't marry me for love. He married me to get his U.S. Citizenship. He used me. He used my family. He used all of us – even IVF, even our beautiful offspring – for himself. His narcissistic, self-absorbed, and distorted self.

The man I met on the mission trip. The Senior Pastor. The Liar. The Loser. An example of Dr. Jekyll and Mr. Hyde. A wolf in sheep's clothing. A fake. A fraud. A false prophet.

The full picture stood before me. He had been engaging in secret, intimate acts with other women. Not once. Not accidentally. Repeatedly. Willingly. Cruelly. It wasn't just sex. It was the deception. The Knowing. The effort it took for him to lie, to come home to us and carry on like nothing was going on. My home, our bed, my trust – all defiled.

Underneath it all, a quiet simmering uproar began to rise. Because this wasn't a mistake. It was his choice. He chose to do this repeatedly. He chose to betray my body, his body, his soul, and my trust – all buried under layers of lies.

April Fool's Day

D – Day had arrived. It was Wednesday, April 1st, and this wasn't a joke. Akuma had left for work early in the morning, and as soon as he left, I had reinforcements come in: Aster and her closest allies, who had become my friends over the last several months after they volunteered to help with my babies. I had the two regular Mom of Multiples moms come to help. I had my army. My support team. My calvary. The moms of multiples were assigned to baby duty; Aster and all her friends were on packing boxes duty, and I was the director of sorts to pull it all off. My support team was armed with boxes, packing tape, and I had a black permanent marker to mark all the boxes with. I wanted to throw all the boxes on the curb, yet when I spoke with my mentor and close ally the day before, she advised me, "Akuma is obviously an incredibly broken person to do all that he did. Let's give some grace."

Grace? Grace after all he had done? I wanted to hurt him.

It took some coaxing and a walk around the neighborhood to finally agree to the idea of grace. I decided to show grace, since he was officially the breadwinner, and I was staying home to nurture and tend to our children.

I wasn't working. How could I, after all I went through physically with the delivery of the triplets? Financially, what would be the point of working when it was less expensive to take care of the triplets myself than to pay over $4,000 a month in childcare; I don't have the money to dish out like that on a former teacher's salary.

I decided he needed to go to work. He needed to know where all his things were, so I would give him some grace and mark each box with a black permanent indicating where all of his belongings were located in each box.

We packed, taped, and labeled all the things that contained Akuma's belongings. We placed everything in the garage, where it was out of sight, and out of mind until evening.

The plan for later was to have my spiritual support team upstairs keeping the babies quiet, fed, and looked after. The divorce papers were ready to be served. Everything was set. Akuma would be coming home that evening.

The Confrontation

Akuma pulled up to the house curbside and walked through the back door roughly around five o'clock in the afternoon. I watched him walk into the bathroom to wash his face, hoping he would come clean with everything he had put me through. He walked out and sat down at our round table to pray with me. After we prayed, I told Akuma I had some things to share with him. He was all ears all of a sudden.

"Akuma, I have some important things to share with you," I spoke strongly.

"Ah…what is it? You can tell me. What's going on?" he asked acting like he cared.

"Well, it's just best I show you. Can you tell me who this is?" I asked as I showed him the profile picture of SugarNSpicy.

He put his head down in shame, guilt, or sadness, knowing he had been found out.

"Listen, I can explain this," he said quietly, with anticipation. "I started speaking with her a couple of months ago."

"No, Akuma. You are lying. Please tell me the truth," I insisted.

"Okay, well…I started talking with her a couple of weeks ago, honest," he fibbed again.

"No, you are lying again. Why is it so hard to tell the truth, Akuma?" I voiced with frustration.

"I swear, Del. I am telling the truth." He continued to lie in my face.

"No, Akuma. You spoke with SugarNSpicy on Sunday. I know this for a fact," the words were blunt and articulate as they came out of my mouth.

Akuma looked up like a lost puppy.

"You know how I know? I am her. She is me. I am SugarNSpicy," I spoke as if glass had shattered all around us.

I continued with my discussion, moving on.

"Can you explain the boysenberry syrup and why it was in your black work bag?" The words were piercing and came out with restraint.

"Oh… the syrup. Yeah, I have been using the syrup when I go over to Jack's sometimes. He makes me pancakes for breakfast when we get together."

His excuses couldn't be lousier and more despicable.

"You're the first guy in all my life who brings his own toothpaste, toothbrush, and a full unopened bottle of boysenberry syrup for guys nights out or in," I thought.

"You must be joking, right? You cannot be serious?" I asked with sarcasm.

"Yes, we eat pancakes together."

Unbelievable.

I am not worth telling the truth to.

Next question.

"Okay, let's move on to this. Please explain why you are taking these pills. Why are there only eight pills left?" I asked maintaining my tense stance.

I thought he would have to let the deck of cards fall on this one. How do you get out of taking pills for one desire alone?

"Oh, yeah, my pills. You know since I am older than you, it actually helps with my blood circulation throughout my body," he earnestly answered.

"Blood circulation?" I questioned him abruptly.

"Yes, I use it for blood circulation," he candidly said.

"Akuma…I wasn't born yesterday. Those pills have one purpose and one purpose only. It's blood circulation directly to your…" I vociferated with conviction.

"No, here, let me show you," he jumped up, as if the bottle would tell a different story.

Akuma proceeded to walk into our bedroom to "show me" what the bottle does. However, when we approached the bedroom closet and he opened it up, it opened to an empty space with nothing in it except a few bare hangers and a shoe rack.

"Where's my stuff?" he wondered.

"Your stuff is in the garage, in boxes. You are leaving here tonight. You will not be living here anymore. Here… hold on…I will be right back," I stood my ground.

I asked Loren to come downstairs and serve Akuma the divorce papers.

He was served without incident. He didn't want to see his children, or run into my support team upstairs, so he walked out like a coward to the side of the house, pulled our car around to the driveway, and collected his belongings out of the garage.

I noticed he stripped our car clean of the bucket car seats.

I'm pretty sure he didn't want his cheap sex dates to see he had babies to take care of. What a joke!

Everyone inside kissed my babies goodnight, gave me some hugs, and prayed one final prayer over my family.

An Atmosphere of Solitude and Peace

This was the first night I was truly alone in my home. The sheer solitude was overwhelmingly sweet. It was the first time I felt peace within and all around me, in what felt like years, after months of abuse.

Even though it was nighttime outside, it felt like sunshine had burst through every room and every crevice in my home. The air was still around me – finally, I felt safe and secure. I could breathe deeply now. I could exhale.

I knew I was strong enough to do this on my own. Honestly, I had been doing it on my own since the near-death delivery. I had overcome so much. I knew the journey would have its ups and downs, but I knew I was stronger for it.

Shortly after he left, I posted a note on my social media page to share that I was going through some hard things, but I had no idea what I would encounter in the years to come. This is what I wrote:

> Lord, thank you for this trial. For it is building
> my character and it's helping your light shine
> upon me to reach those I love and beyond.
> For your grace is sufficient for me. I love you.

Over the next few weeks, I continued to communicate with Akuma about the triplets and what they were up to. This was the only year of "firsts", and I still wanted him to be a part of it – he was their dad, after all.

Uneasy Realities

I was in a place of embarrassment and worry when I scheduled an appointment with my family doctor to get tested for HIV/AIDS and sexually transmitted diseases.

Even though we had been intimate only once since the triplets were born, I wanted to take every precaution to keep myself safe. Thankfully, every test came back negative for any disease or condition. It was an embarrassing and emotionally draining story to share.

I quickly learned that when getting a divorce in Colorado, if you have children, both parents must attend a four-hour parenting class. I had an issue with this, as I was still not getting great sleep throughout the nights and I could not foresee myself taking a four-hour parenting class on top of continuing to do all the parental duties on my own.

Mentally and emotionally, I had been drained from it all. Everything I went through in just six months had me struggling to focus solely on myself. I was in survivor mode, and if I could eliminate the stress of something I knew I couldn't handle at the time – it was the divorce.

Shortly before my first Mother's Day, the divorce papers were dismissed. I needed to focus on my continued health. I had several physical health issues that I still struggled with postpartum. My plantar fasciitis had gotten more severe. The custom-made shoe inserts were no longer helping, so I got rid of those.

I started going to nail salons when I could afford to get pedicures so an attendant could rub my feet. I continued to see a massage therapist regularly working on my back and my feet. Nothing helped and it was so painful to walk, stand, and move around. I walked in pain. I carried the triplets with pain. I did everything in pain.

I suffered with pain from my spinal block. Standing for more than thirty minutes would put so much stress on my back and body. I would often bend over and lay my hands on the floor to get a good stretch. Sitting for more than thirty minutes at a time was painful as well. My daily chores of tending to my children came with struggle - mentally, emotionally, and physically.

The task of motherhood had taken a toll on me. I had no time to grieve my marriage. There was no time to think about it with all the things I had to do for my babies. I wanted them to enjoy their childhood, so I always put them first. My pain had to wait – Scarlett, Kingston and Reece were my greatest blessings, and I wanted them to remember that. I wanted them to say – my mom did everything for us.

Akuma made little to no effort once I asked him to leave on April Fool's Day. He agreed to come over one week from 5 a.m. to 9 a.m. in early June, so I could get four hours of uninterrupted sleep and so I could function during the day and through the night shift on my own.

By June, I had regular help who came almost every day to help me with the triplets. I was involved in my church with some fun family groups, where I was able to make new friends and get a small break from all the chaos that surrounded me.

My First Break

A family that volunteered often to tend to my motherly duties gifted me five whole days away from my children to go explore the mountains surrounding our beautiful state with my friend Faith. It was my first actual break from the triplets in over seven months. A break where I could sleep in, relax, laugh, enjoy the summer, sunsets, sunrises, fun road trips with loud music, hot coffee, and good food. It was everything I wanted and needed for months on end.

This sweet family also pitched in from their own pockets and time with a complimentary professional photoshoot of my sweet loves while I was away.

Lisa surprised me in July with these gorgeous photographs of my family from when she watched them in June. It was the kindest, most loving gesture I had seen from someone other than my family in months. It meant the world to me.

My first summer was spent with family and friends. We went to birthday parties, spent time in the backyard, explored new things, and I watched the triplets grow.

More Abuse and Unkept Accountability

The summer months were also a time of more pain and abuse that occurred when I was either resting from it all or making formula and grocery runs for my family. When I wasn't present, while my help was there and Akuma would be doing his parenting time with the kids, he would make horrific comments and utterances about me as an individual and as a mother, such as:

"Adele is so incompetent and crazy. I have to do everything because she can't."

"Adele needs to change her clothes and clean herself up. She doesn't look presentable to us."

"I'm (Akuma) such an amazing dad. I'm an expert at raising kids. Adele doesn't know what she is doing as a mother."

"I (Akuma) never wanted these kids in the first place. This was all Del's idea."

"Adele reminds me of the Nazis in Germany. She doesn't talk to the babies during their feedings or when she changes their diapers during naptime. The Nazis did that, and the babies all died."

"Adele doesn't need to eat that. She is fat already."

"Why do you always ask how Adele is doing? What about me (Akuma)? No one ever asks how I am doing?"

"When is Adele going to start being their mom?"

"The babies always sleep when I'm (Akuma) here and they never cry in front of me."

The verbal abuse was so profound, and now, the help I had experienced his abuse as well.

By late June, my mentor Nancy helped me fund the ability for Akuma to attend an "Every Man's Battle" conference, and I noticed a glimmer of hope after he returned from the event. He was brutally honest with me about several things. He shared with me how he had adulterous affairs behind my back while we struggled getting pregnant, during my pregnancy, and after the birth. He told me he hired an escort and how they met at a hotel to have sex. He was on three dating websites looking for sex only. He let me check his phone. He had an accountability group. He was reading his Bible. He was going to church.

Two weeks later, we met for lunch, and I asked to do a random phone check – he was reluctant and chose not to let me check.

A few days later, a friend taught me how to look up his phone history and track his location and how long he had been in one location versus another.

The following day, Akuma was over at the house to see the kids and I asked him if I could do a random phone check. He allowed me to look, and I chose to do a location search. He lied about not going out late, and I discovered more evidence of sexual misconduct. This man could not be trusted. I knew then I could no longer be his wife. The only question remained was whether he could be a present parent.

At the end of July, I had a long discussion with my mom, and I spoke with Akuma afterward. My mom and I made the ultimate sacrifice to bring Akuma back into the house momentarily. He was living with someone I knew and trusted, so most of his belongings stayed with our mutual friend. I told Akuma he needed to be here to experience everything it took to be a dad and be present daily for the triplets.

I knew his presence would be vital to the triplets' development, and I wanted each of them to have a relationship with their dad – because all things aside – the triplets had nothing to do with his shortcomings and bad behavior. They deserved to have a father.

In early August, Akuma moved back in. I didn't expect date nights or attempt to keep him accountable. I stopped doing phone checks. I was done trying to be his wife.

He never wanted one.

All he wanted was U.S. citizenship.

What I did expect was for him to be fully present for his kids, that he would be honest and truthful for their sake. I asked him to let me know when he was at work and when he would be home.

In September, I set up some parameters with our family vehicle that Akuma drove. I had a tracker put on our car without his knowledge. Since we were still married, it was legal, so I took every precaution to make sure my children were safe – since Akuma's track record wasn't kid-friendly.

I wanted to make sure when we got divorced, and if I needed to, to prove without a doubt whether Akuma should have access for overnights with our precious cargo or no time unsupervised with our kids at all.

By the end of September and into early October, the tracker allowed me to see that Akuma could not be trusted as he would say he was at work; when in reality, he was at the movies or Dave & Busters. He would say he was on his way home, and he would be driving around in circles. The tracker proved Akuma had no desire to help with the triplets. There were times he would say he was stuck in traffic and would be driving up and down the main street from our house for over an hour to get out of putting the kids to sleep. Akuma's lifestyle told all. He was selfish. A true covert narcissist and the only person who mattered was himself.

I put Akuma on a shelf to attend to later.

The Triplet's First Birthday

It was October. The triplets' first birthday was fast approaching, and I wanted to make it incredibly special. I had been planning their birthday for months. I purchased these adorable handmade hats from Etsy for them to wear. The hats were specific to their favorite colors and the colors of their bed sheets – pops of color in every hat. I decorated their highchairs with multi-colored ribbons and had cut out cardstock paper to spell O-N-E, a letter for each highchair. I purchased tubs of our favorite ice cream – Oreos and Cream, Strawberry, and Vanilla. I invited over sixty volunteers for the October Sunday Sundae Social to celebrate Reece, Scarlett, and Kingston.

Everything was perfect; it was the most beautiful October day. The triplets were celebrated by so many. My friends celebrated me too.

"Del, Titus and I bought this champagne for you! You made it through this year! We are so proud of you and love you so much!" Faith and Titus joyfully cheered.

We ended the night laying each triplet in their bedtime footed pajamas next to their preemie outfits they wore in the NICU. The difference a year made was astonishing. Reece, Scarlett and Kingston were once so tiny, barely the length of my forearm, wrapped in wires and swaddled in hope.

Their first days were marked by quiet beeps and careful whispers. Little hands curled into the smallest fist imaginable. But over the months, they bloomed. Every ounce gained was a victory, every milestone a celebration. Crawling at nine months and walking by eleven. Kingston, Reece and Scarlett didn't follow the rules of the adjusted age. They were each stepping into their own – advanced, absolutely gorgeous and strong.

Now, at one year old – they were unrecognizable from that fragile preemie state – each cheek, round and kissable, their big brown eyes bright with curiosity, and their sweet voices and giggles filled the room like music. Their once delicate bodies now burst with energy, and every smile is proof of their tremendous growth, resilience and irresistible cuteness they've carried from their very first breath.

An Outlet to Give Back

After the triplets' birthday, I let Akuma know we were not going to be a family anymore, and he needed to start looking for his own place. I let him know he could stay through Christmas to spend one last Christmas together as a family.

I needed an outlet for my stressful life. I desired to be around adults and not just the volunteers who helped me with the triplets. For several months, Akuma made me feel worthless and like someone who had no value. I began to tell others, "I was just a mom" because I currently couldn't work, mostly because of all my health issues, but also raising toddler triplets was no easy feat.

I contacted Piper, my primary NICU nurse, about volunteering as a cuddler in the NICU at RMHC. She got me set up with the hospital chaplain to attend a class about the process and the application to start.

I started sometime in late 2015 into 2016. I had one shift on Sundays from 12 p.m. to 3 p.m. in the afternoon. I loved every minute of it. It was a quiet place where I worked alongside many of the nurses who loved on my babies, held precious children with critical needs, folded preemie clothes, and contributed to our community. I always loved giving back, and this gave me a significant sense of pride in doing something more than just being the "triplet mom".

Health Concerns

November brought up some health issues for Kingston. He had one visit to the ED at the end of August for respiratory issues, and since he was under two years of age, he needed to continue to be watched. This was his second time in just under three months of returning to the ED for more respiratory issues.

By January of 2016, I knew I would be refiling for divorce. I needed to establish medical care for the children and their future wellness visits. At the time, I had dual coverage, and with the divorce evident, I knew I would only be on Medicaid. I had to find a new doctor and find one quickly. Finding a family doctor to take Medicaid was one issue; finding a doctor who was taking on new Medicaid patients was nearly impossible.

I walked the floors of several adjacent hospital buildings asking for assistance. I nearly gave up after having over seven doors slam in my face saying "no" until I found one that would take all three of my kids. I asked if they could take me in as a patient, and I received a "No." I figured if my kids can be seen for their needs, this is what mattered. Even though I was having several health issues, I put my own needs aside because they were my priority.

My baby boy, Kingston, returned to the ED at the end of January for yet another respiratory issue, lots of wheezing, and accelerated breathing.

In February, Kingston returned to the ED for a fever of 103.6 and an ear infection. His ED visits began to become a trend. I began recognizing the pediatric doctors and nurses in the hospital so well, I thought maybe I should work there. Everyone was so helpful and kind to both of us as we became regular visitors.

His Departure

In March, Akuma officially moved out. He got his own apartment and even shared pictures with me of what it looked like. He seemed somewhat proud of his new freedom. He didn't look like a family man, and his new apartment looked like a bachelor pad. Nothing about his new digs disclosed he had a child, let alone three. In Akuma fashion, he refused to tell me exactly where this apartment was located.

A Desire to Feel the Sunshine

On Friday, April 8th, I was determined to get outside and get some exercise. I decided my plantar fasciitis wasn't going to get in the way of getting some sunshine and some fresh air. I attempted to run, and I realized quickly I pushed myself too hard and by Saturday afternoon something didn't feel right.

On Sunday, April 10th, I drove down to RMHC for my cuddler shift. I had parked my car, and once I got off the elevator to the NICU floor, I realized I could barely walk, and I began to grip the railings with both hands. I ended up calling the NICU nurse station to get assistance as I had lost my ability to walk.

"Hey Adele, what's going on?" a nurse asked as she met me with a wheelchair.

"Hey, sorry about that. I'm not sure what is going on. I tried to run on Friday afternoon and I think, maybe, I pushed myself too hard. I was able to walk yesterday. I always have pain when I walk, but now I can't walk at all for some reason," I graciously answered.

"Okay, well, we are at the hospital. How about I just wheel you down to the ED?" she giggled as I laughed with her.

"Sounds like a plan!" I laughed back.

I took some tests and discovered I developed a stress fracture in my knee. The ED doctor encouraged me to use crutches for four to six weeks along with being on bed rest to heal the stress fracture.

I reached out to Akuma the same day I came home from the ED.

"Hey, Akuma. I developed a stress fracture in my knee, and I was informed to be on bed rest and to use crutches for four to six weeks. I wanted you to know, as I could use your help around the house as 1) chasing toddlers while using crutches would be challenging and 2) I need to rest," I communicated to him via text.

"I don't believe you. I'm not coming," his response was quick and short.

Sadly, after this stress fracture, I informed the hospital chaplain I could no longer return due to too many health challenges and little to no help from my estranged husband.

I filed for divorce at the end of April, and my lawyer was on top of everything. She made sure to check all the boxes and thought of things I didn't know to think of. Charlotte came with me to one of my divorce meetings with my lawyer to help give support and advice through the process. Her support was important to me during this time.

After everything I went through with Akuma, I wanted to make sure my triplets could benefit the best from what had occurred. The triplets needed to be looked after. It was a full-time job, and Akuma was utterly incapable of doing this task. He lacked in every area. He could not be responsible enough to save his life. I wanted to make sure the triplets were safe and secure.

Over the course of April and May, Akuma came up with excuse after excuse for why he couldn't "show up" and be an active parent for his kids. What started as begging to see the "firsts" of the triplets' life was short-lived after I completed the four-hour parenting class in May.

"Good evening, parents, thank you for attending this class tonight for your upcoming divorce proceedings. My colleague and I will walk you through each page in the workbook. If you happen to have any questions, please ask. That is what we are here for. Please sign your name on the attendance sheet as it is being passed around…okay, please open your workbook up to page one," the instructor announced.

"Good evening, Sir, on the parenting time section, I have a question. What if you have to beg the other parent to spend time with your children?" I questioned with great concern.

"Ms. Charles, thank you for your question. Sadly, if you have to beg for the other parent to participate, I don't think he wants to be there. If I were you, I would stop begging him to show up," he responded.

June 3, 2016

Off of a whim, Akuma had planned along with me to see the kids on Friday, June 3, 2016, at Congress Park. I made sure the kids were safe and had asked my mentor, Nancy, who helped teach me the lesson of grace to him, to meet me at the park that day to stand off in the distance to make sure he didn't do anything to harm the triplets.

I bent down to the red triplet wagon once I settled them all into their seats and told them, "Today, you are going to see daddy."

The triplets looked at me in wonder as if to ask, "*Who is that*?" I discerned worry from each of their faces about being around Akuma. I attempted to reassure each of them it was okay, and mommy wouldn't be far away.

Akuma took them to a shaded tree area and played with the triplets for up to an hour. At the end of the visit, I took some pictures of the triplets with him and forwarded them to his phone to have the memory of being with them.

Shortly after, I met up with Nancy to see what she observed about the visit.

"I noticed he was playing games with the kids and made a game of chase. The boys seemed fine, yet Scarlett, I noticed she was actually running and trying to get away from him. I saw her screaming and crying. Just look at Scarlett's face – she is distraught," she shuddered.

"Oh my goodness, yes, I see it in her eyes. Her eyes are filled with tears," I noted.

"Oh, Del, let's cheer up these darlings. Let me buy them some popsicles," she added.

It was as if Scarlett's eyes had become fragile glass, each blink threatening to spill shimmering tears gathering in the corners. The hurt in Scarlett's eyes were unmistakable – raw, unspoken, and deeper than any words could capture. They told a silent story of ache, making my heart tighten just to witness it. I took a picture to remember this moment, and for several days following this event, Scarlett seemed to hurt. Her face told it all.

How to Spot a Neglectful Dad

From July to December of 2016, Akuma decided to not pay any child support. He never communicated with me about his whereabouts or where he was working. Akuma's true colors started to unravel on the day of the triplets' birth, and it continued to unravel every day, every week and every month following.

Each onion layer displayed a consistent pattern – consistent absences, emotional neglect, broken promises, financial irresponsibility, zero communication, avoidance of parental responsibilities and towards me: failure to co-parent, blame-shifting, withholding support for punishment, conflict-stirring, disrespect, and undermining, and avoiding accountability.

Those months leading up to the divorce were like raising children with a ghost who still cast shadows. The triplets learned early on not to depend on Akuma for anything, as if asking him to show up was requesting too much. He didn't just neglect the role of being a father – he weaponized it.

Akuma had made plans to visit the triplets on August 29th as well. I learned early on not to depend on him for anything either, and I made sure to never tell the kids he made plans to see them, for this very reason. I took the kids to the park he suggested on a specific day at a specific time, and he never showed up. No call, no text, nothing.

Because I never said anything to the children, I didn't have to deal with disappointed faces and tears. It was just a time when the kids and I went out to play. I made it a habit to protect my kids. Regrettably, I had to protect them from their own father.

I had learned leading up to the divorce the only reason Akuma had made plans to see the kids was because a Child and Family Investigator informed him to do so. Because the triplets were under the age of two, we had a CFI involved in our divorce case. I didn't realize what a blessing this was at the time, yet I am incredibly thankful there was a CFI involved.

The CFI was responsible for holding interviews between the two of us and was to do a home visit with each of us as well as make recommendations with the Court for the best interests of the children. I realized this was my time to shine for the CFI and the Family Court system.

These were the findings the CFI wrote in her report:

- To date, the father has participated very little. He had one office meeting, but the CFI has not heard from him since and his phone has been disconnected.
- The undersigned does not see support, commitment of shared values – mostly because of the father's basic abandonment of the children. He doesn't visit, rarely checks in, and has no involvement.
- Mother is an amazing mother. The CFI expected to see a house full of chaos, but she is so organized – on top of everything. She has charts, cubbies, bins – everything to keep her organized and she seems to bubble with energy and excitement. She loves being

a mother, and the triplets were all over her with hugs and happiness.

- The children have the support of their mother and her friends and relatives. That connection is very important to the children.
- The CFI has absolutely no concerns with the mother's ability to do this. Based on the father's lack of involvement with the children, it is clear that the father doesn't even understand the emotional needs of the children.

The CFI recommended the Court to follow a specific format for parenting time with Akuma. This is what she wrote in her report:

It is difficult to come up with a schedule for father and children based on his recent history. The CFI feels it is best to propose a step-up plan that **requires him to comply with each stage before increasing time** unless parties agree otherwise. The undersigned realizes this is fairly restrictive, but the CFI feels the father needs to **prove some commitment to the children**. Thus the CFI recommends that father have parenting time with the children as follows:

1. Supervised visits once a week for 3 hours for 6 weeks. These visits should be supervised by a mutually agreed upon person or father can use a professional supervisor and be responsible for those expenses. The date/time to be agreed upon by the parents.

2. Supervised visits twice a week for 3 hours for 8 weeks.
3. Monitored visits twice a week for 6 hours for 8 weeks.
4. Unsupervised visits twice a week for 6 hours for 8 weeks.
5. Unsupervised visits twice a week for a full day i.e. 9:00 a.m. – 6:00 p.m. for 3 months.

- After the father completes this stepped-up plan, the parties should meet with a mediator to discuss further increases in father's parenting time for when the children turn three.
- As a condition of father's parenting time, Father needs to have his own supplies, clothing, toys, diapers, and food for the children for all parenting time along with appropriate accommodations.
- The mother brings the children to the visits and picks them up until the visits are no longer supervised.
- Before the father is allowed to take the children to his home, he needs to provide documentation of the home, including pictures to prove it is reasonably appropriately equipped for the children.
- In the event the children become sick or injured, either parent may take the children in for urgent

care but should notify the other parent as soon as possible.

- It does not seem appropriate to suggest a holiday schedule at this point, not knowing the father's commitment to the children.
- Each parent should inform the other parent of any changes of business/employment or residential address and/or phone number within 48 hours of the change.

These were most of the major concerns the CFI found of great importance in preparation of our divorce. The Judge added every single one to our permanent parenting plan and he also included that if Akuma does not complete the step-up plan as specifically set forth herein or misses parenting time, the step he is currently in shall restart from the beginning until successful completion.

Objection: To His Own Foolishness

This was the happiest day of my life since the birth of my triplets; it was the day of my divorce. It was also a day of great humor, all brought on by Akuma.

My lawyer and I came prepared.

Akuma was there by himself. He didn't have a single person there to support him or provide him with a positive witness statement. The few friends he had, left him after discovering what he had done to his children and me.

My friend Faith and my mom were there to show support, and my mom was there to testify on my behalf. The hearing was scheduled to be all day, from nine o'clock in the morning to four o'clock in the afternoon.

The Judge seemed to read between the lines regarding Akuma's behavior and ridiculous requests to the Court. Akuma was up to his tactics again. It was a sight to see. Akuma had requested to have a Spanish interpreter during our divorce, even though he was fluent in English and requested my mom to leave the room as he told the Judge he would be unable to proceed with the hearing if she was present.

We had to wait 45 minutes for two interpreters to be present. They had to alternate with any hearing for over an hour to maintain quality and had to alternate every thirty to forty-five minutes to speak on Akuma's behalf. The current interpreter was the only one in the building that day.

The fact that Akuma needed an interpreter after working in the U.S. and in the V.I. where the primary language spoken is English, suggests he was causing a disruption or attempting to have the case postponed. My guess is he needed to feel powerful today in the courtroom. He tried to control everything and he tried to convince us otherwise.

I gave the first testimony of everything from my name and address to sharing how Akuma became a US Citizen to the birth of our triplets, the recommendations of the CFI regarding the parenting plan that we both agreed upon and everything else.

During the hearing, Akuma was to use a headset, so he could understand what the interpreter was saying as my testimony was shared.

He never wore the headset.

Not because it didn't fit, but because he could clearly understand English.

How do you propose and marry me knowing I barely speak Spanish, and all of a sudden – you can't speak English at all or understand it? What a fool.

The Judge even addressed him in court about it, "Well, you don't have to take your headphones off. She'll (the interpreter) say everything."

My lawyer had asked if Akuma had set up parenting time with the kids and when the last time he saw them. He did tell the Court he had not seen them for over three months. We had no way of contacting him as his phone was disconnected and he refused to communicate with me of his whereabouts.

I had done all the mandatory paperwork with regard to the courts and provided them with evidence showing I was not employed since June of 2014 due to a high-risk pregnancy and orders from my OB to take it easy. I haven't looked for work since, as I've been caring of the triplets full-time.

Due to Akuma's continued lack of support or care of the needs of the triplets, I began getting food stamps early after the birth of the triplets. We were on a program called WIC, Women Infants and Children, where I was provided monthly help for each triplet in regard to formula, bread, eggs, milk, peanut butter, a small allowance of fresh fruit and vegetables, cheese, yogurt, beans, certain types of juice, baby food and baby cereal.

After the triplets turned one, the triplets' WIC diet also had a prescription of PediSure to continue to help them grow and develop. I had regular meetings with the WIC office to update the growth, diet, and any concerns I had.

As hard as it was to be added to Medicaid, WIC, and food stamps for me, I knew without the assistance I would never have been able to care for the triplets without the help. My case worker, Gracie, was the perfect helper for me. She was gentle and understanding.

Being on assistance, knowing my background in schooling, brought me to my knees, and I cried several times about having to be on government assistance to care for my family. I was embarrassed by this, and it was something I never opened up about with family or friends. It made me feel like a failure. I never imagined my life was going to be like this, yet I am incredibly grateful for a program like this for families who depend on it to feed their family, tend to their medical emergencies and care – to help families in great need.

Akuma could not acknowledge all the expenses spoken in testimony for the care of the triplets in regard to eating more, paying for clothing and shoes, grooming, diapers, toys, and gifts.

He tried over and over while I was giving my testimony to interrupt and give his own objection, *in English.* There were several objections spoken by my lawyer about Akuma trying to present his own testimony, *in English*, and the Judge had to explain court procedures to Akuma time and time again.

The Court: The procedure, sir, is that if you have an objection to the exhibit, you can do that. There really isn't so far as I've heard at this point any basis for an objection to this testimony because this is testimony of what the Petitioner's costs are for the care of the children…so it's important to understand that you don't get to testify during cross-examination.

So I'd encourage you to write things down. And whenever you hear that she testifies and you think, "Well, that's not right, and I'll prove it," you'll have that opportunity when it's your turn to testify or when you cross-examine her. So long as it's the form of a question. Do you have a pad and paper?

Akuma: I – I have one, Your Honor.

My lawyer continued to ask questions about splitting up the assets and liabilities between us. Akuma was already behind in child support totaling around $2,400.00. My offer was to collect his entire retirement fund and the vehicle we shared in lieu of receiving spousal maintenance.

My Lawyer: And - - and why do you believe that that's fair?

Me: I believe it is fair because in my past and being married to Mr. Campbell, he has the tendency to run from his problems, and my fear is that I will not receive maintenance, that I will not receive any child support. My fear is that he will leave the country. My fear is that I will never receive any kind of money to go towards the care of our triplets.

At the time, Akuma claimed to be making only $2K a month, so for his three triplet toddlers I would only receive $696.00 a month going forward. Per our permanent order we were to annually exchange income information, tax returns, and paystubs so I could remain informed of his income, and when I began working, I could do the same.

The Court gave Akuma his time to cross-examine me and made sure he understood that he was to ask questions, not give a story or tell his version of the facts.

Once again, Akuma proved he knew the English language as he chose to cross-examine me in *English only*, while the Spanish Interpreter stood there, probably wondering why she and the other Spanish Interpreter were present. What a waste of Court resources and time.

He gave up his right to testify as he probably never wanted my lawyer to cross examine him, and we proceeded to closing remarks.

Akuma: It seems to be that when you sit over this side of the table, it's - - you shed tears. And I - - I just want to thank the Court, first of all, for their time and your patience and their - - for judging this case, you know, in a fair way that - - and explain to me many points that I consider really important in this case or relevant. I feel that at times I might receive too much information. Maybe I'm not used to it, but, anyway, today I'm just going to say this. I'm tired. I don't want to fight anymore. I - - when I say fight, I'm talking about proceeding with this case. And I - - I would - -yeah, I said tired - - I mean I can accept the financial proposal - - financial agreement that was proposed, and I just want to finish with this. Yeah, I just want to move on. One thing that I have learned is to respect every person, every human being. And I just want to finish on that note. I have never raised my voice, any word - - any offensive word towards the other party, and it'll always be that way. She's the mother of my children. Yeah, I'm going to do what's possible to build a relationship with my children as long as the Petitioner allows it. She can obtain the vehicle. And whatever, Judge, you decide what I should do. I have always been an exemplary citizen, and I'll continue being one. Thank you very much.

My Lawyer's Final Remarks: Your Honor, at the end of the day, this case is about really three young children. They're not even two years old yet. With all due respect, Mr. Campbell remarked that he's tired. The person who's probably the most tired is Ms. Charles, who has been tasked with caring for these three children by herself every day and every night. It is unrefuted based on the testimony here that Mr. Campbell has not complied with the court orders. He has not provided adequate financial disclosures in a timely manner. He did not respond to discovery. It has been delay after delay that has caused anxiety and delay in this case to Ms. Charles that affects these three children. Mr. Campbell, it is unrefuted, has all but abandoned these children. He has not seen them since June. He has made little to no effort to inquire about their health or wellbeing unless or until Ms. Charles, their mother, reaches out to him to inform them of medical issues.

Ms. Charles testified she doesn't even have a way at this point in time to communicate with him regularly because his cell phone has been disconnected, and if he has a new one, he has not provided that information. It is also unrefuted that he has failed to pay any child support whatsoever, even dollar one to Ms. Charles for two - - for the past two months and that previously was $400 short.

So what we know is that these children are going to be loved. They're going to be supported. We know that because Ms. Charles testified to it and her mother, the - - the children's maternal grandmother testified that, you know, she is there and they have the family support to meet these children's needs, but by no means does the law of Colorado suggest that it is a grandparent's responsibility or anyone extended in the family's responsibility to financially support three children that these parties chose to bring into the world.

So with regard to the other outstanding issues, we do ask the parenting plan be adopted as an order of court. With regard to the financial issues, my comments are, if Mr. Campbell is agreeing to the proposals, the Court can take that into consideration to the extent that those assets and those values are accurate.

The court abided by everything we requested during the hearing and every recommendation given by the CFI, plus the one he added about returning to a step if it wasn't completed in full. I was awarded full decision-making on everything related to the children – what school they would attend as they got older, what dentist or doctor they would see, when we would take a vacation, or if there were any more medical emergencies.

The Judge also said that if Akuma was off on child support at all, even a dollar, he would not be able to claim them as dependents on his income tax return.

After the divorce was settled, I went to dinner with my close friends, and we then proceeded to celebrate my divorce downtown. It truly ended up being the best day ever. *Celebrating my divorce!*

Spiritual Direction

Over the course of October and November, I still hadn't received child support and began to feel weary. I was meeting with a Christian spiritual director at the time, who was helping me work through several issues postpartum and post-divorce. My spiritual director helped guide me through my relationship with God and helped me discern God's presence and will for my life.

I had a lot of anger from everything I went through; I felt abandoned and rejected for so long. The spiritual director was able to capture deeply personal and many vulnerable moments in my life. She gave me a blend of introspection and hope and helped me work through several fears I held inside.

One of my biggest fears was doing this alone. Who would want to raise triplets with me, knowing they weren't their own children? Would I ever get remarried? Who would want this life with me?

During one spiritual exercise, she asked me to think of a word to share during our next session in December. I came up with the word, "First" and wrote a poem from it.

First

You are my first
My beloved
I've plotted out each day before you

Run to me when you are weary
Look to me when the tide takes you under

Life doesn't have to be this difficult
I'll catch you when you fall
You are a strong woman to go through what
You are going through

You don't have to stand on only your two feet
I've surrounded you with angels that will look after you
I've provided them for you
Each one is a glimpse of my glory

I have looked after you and will continue to do so
Believe in me
Have faith in me

I will never let you down

Continue to seek after me in your prayers
Wait on me
I will answer your call
Be still and know that I am God
Holy and omnipotent
Faithful and full of grace

*

Lord Jesus, I come to you
I surrender everything I need to you
I cannot do this task alone
I am burdened – drowning in trying to figure this all out
Forgive me for having little faith
For I know you created this vastly beautiful place
And you take the time to look after the little sparrow
Nothing is too difficult for you
Nothing is impossible for you
You are the King of Kings, and you have overcome the world

I believe that you will provide
I believe that you will have my family in your precious
and mighty hands
You will not allow this situation to rob me of my joy
To rob me of my faith

All along, you have reminded me

I AM YOUR BELOVED
I am yours and you are mine
The apple of thine eyes
You brought me out of the darkness and into the glorious light
You took this barren woman and blessed my womb three times over
You have met me in the darkest of times and have blessed my life over and over
Miracles all around
You set me free
You continue to search after me
For you want me to cling to you, your heart and place every dream, every tear,
every thought into the realms of your love

You seek all of me
You want to see me…whole
Solely dependent on you

Written by Adele Charles, November 25 and 27, 2016

Answers to Prayer

On December 6, 2016, I finally received my first child support payment along with other financial support from the court order.

For Christmas, a section leader from our church set up this Christmas Box to gift two single moms with the blessings of love and care for children. I was one of those single moms. We were so blessed to receive such kindness from families and complete strangers who didn't know me, but only the story the section leaders shared about us.

My precious friends Shelly and Rich wrote this in a newsletter they sent out, "Imagine giving birth to triplets. Then imagine raising them all by yourself because the father wanted no part of you or raising three young lives. To make matters worse, you receive no financial support and continue to have health-related issues from the delivery of those tiny little babies." Her letter touched the hearts of so many, and we received a huge blessing on Christmas Eve.

Once I received the money from child support, the financial support and this Christmas blessing, I paid off all my personal debt and was debt-free.

More Health Concerns in the New Year – 2017

In January 2017, I was folding laundry and stood up wrong and ended up straining my back, possibly spraining it. I went to the ED and was referred to Sky Ridge Physical Therapy to work on my back issues. This was the first time I saw a doctor since my ED visit in 2016 when I had a stress fracture in my knee. I did not have a primary care doctor still, so knowing I could at least have my back worked on meant so much to me.

My issues with my feet would have to wait a bit longer than I hoped. Walking daily was still very difficult and painful. I could only wear a certain type of shoe, yet I still walked with great pain.

By March 2017, Kingston had ten ED visits to the doctor from shortly after the NICU in November 2014 up until now. During the summer of 2016, he was diagnosed with RAD – Reactive Airway Disease, the precursor of asthma.

Early on the morning of March 20, I went to get the triplets up from their nighttime sleep to get ready for breakfast. When I walked in their room, I noticed a wretched stench coming from their toddler beds. I thought someone may have thrown up or had diarrhea. The closer I approached their beds, there was no vomit, but I noticed the smell was coming from Kingston.

I ran and got a box of wipes because I knew this would be a heavy-duty clean up. I opened his diaper and noticed something so odd about the contents of his diaper. He had appeared to have diarrhea or poop of some kind, yet it didn't resemble any feces I had ever seen before. It looked like leftover oatmeal. It smelled different and looked very gross. I decided not to throw away the soiled diaper but put all its contents into a Ziploc gallon bag and made a call to the pediatrician for him to be looked at.

After I made arrangements with my other son and daughter, I took Kingston into the Peds office. The doctor took some lab tests and a few stool samples and came back in to meet with me.

"Good day, Ms. Charles, I'm Dr. Grant. I was able to look at the labs, and it looks like Kingston is severely dehydrated. His stool sample came back with blood in it. I am in the process of admitting him to the hospital now, and I will get you and Kingston set up on the PICU floor," she informed me with urgency.

"Wait, what? I didn't bring much in my diaper bag except my phone charger, an extra diaper, and a change of clothes for him. Right now? Are you sure?" I verbalized with concern.

"Yes, I will walk you to the PICU and get you set up in a room. I have already called the PICU floor, and they are waiting for your arrival," she affirmed.

When I reached the floor, they had a special bed set up for toddlers; it looked like a crib, and it had a hospital bed nearby that I could sit and rest upon.

Once we arrived, they had Kingston set up his IV drip to start fluids since he was so dehydrated. They put him in a hospital gown, attached his hospital bracelet, and ran further tests. Shortly after, the floor doctor came in to notify me of his findings.

"Good Day, Ms. Charles. Can I ask you a few questions?" he asked.

"Sure thing," I responded.

"Have you traveled out of the country recently? Or gone anywhere else?" he inquired.

"No, we haven't. At most, we visit the local gym so I can work out. The triplets are in day care while I'm at the gym. I think because of Spring Break, he could have caught something with all the kids being on Spring recess," I answered back.

"Okay, good to know. What he has been diagnosed with is C-Diff, or Clostridium Difficile. Most people get it by traveling to other countries, or it often occurs when adults become elderly. Kingston has also been diagnosed with Rotavirus," he confirmed with me, "C-diff can be fatal if it isn't treated properly within a certain time frame."

Suddenly, a deep wave of fear and worry settled in my chest. My mind instantly leapt to worst-case scenarios, fueled by the unfamiliarity and seriousness of the infection. I could feel my heart race and my stomach knot as I imagined Kingston's discomfort, diarrhea, the severity of dehydration, and his having to be admitted so quickly without much warning.

I knew this was a medical emergency, and I wanted to make sure I followed the orders of the court, so I needed to somehow get in touch with Akuma. The only number I had was from court, and it was his work number.

"Good afternoon, does Akuma Campbell work here?" I asked.

"Yes, he works here. May I ask who is calling?" the man asked.

"Yes, this is his ex-wife, and I wanted to inform him that his son has a medical emergency and is being admitted to the hospital. He is located at Sky Ridge Medical Center. Could you pass the information on to him? Thanks. Bye," I said and hung up the phone.

While waiting to see if Akuma would contact me, I reached out to some family and friends to let them know I would be staying overnight with Kingston. I asked for some help gathering a few more things from home, so I could stay with Kingston and he wouldn't have to be alone with only the medical staff.

About two hours later I got a call from Akuma. I couldn't remember the last time he called me or communicated with me.

"Hello? Yes…Kingston was admitted earlier today. He has two infections. One could potentially be fatal," I explained.

"Okay, I see. I am going to come to the hospital to see him. I will bring a friend with me. Okay?" he said, "I'll be there in an hour, bye."

I couldn't believe my ears. It had been ten whole months since the triplets had seen Akuma. Would he really show up this time? Would Kingston remember him? I wondered what this would be like.

At the time, a mutual acquaintance of ours was in the PICU room visiting Kingston and he assured me I wouldn't be left alone when and if he came to visit. This acquaintance grew up with Akuma, so it would be a reunion for all of us – not a positive one, to say the least.

The hospital staff notified me that Akuma and his friend had arrived. I had them come down to the hallway and walk in when they reached the door.

Akuma opened the door and walked in first.

"Kinggggstonnnn – it's Daddddyyyyy!" he exaggerated.

As soon as Kingston saw him, he astonished me when he rolled his eyes at Akuma. We both took notice of that. How could a two-year-old know what kind of person he was at such a young age?

Akuma proceeded to sit on the hospital bed near our son.

"Kingston, Daddy wants to see you. Kingston, Daddy wants to play with you. Kingston, Daddy wants a high five," he broadcasted.

I was appalled at everything he said, Daddy this and Daddy that. I wasn't sure if he was trying to show off to this lady friend he brought in with him or if he knew our son didn't recognize him.

I could tell Kingston felt very uneasy around Akuma. It was like his instincts kicked in and he knew right away Akuma wasn't a safe person. After Akuma left, it affected Kingston in a negative way. He would tell me he wanted to bite me and hit me; it was so out of character for him to act that way.

Akuma never returned to the hospital to visit our son after that first day. Kingston remained hospitalized for an additional two more nights until we went home on March 22nd.

Unfortunately, from going back home one day while Kingston was hospitalized to grab a few personal items, the C-Diff had affected our family. Scarlett and Reece ended up with C-Diff as well, not as severe as Kingston, yet all three were on a 21-day antibiotic from the compound pharmacy, and I ended up with rotavirus the day we came home from the hospital. At midnight, I checked myself into the ED to get some help with anti-diarrheal meds and some Zofran. The months of March and April were exhausting and trying for all of us.

A Disheartening Request

In early April, I received a call from Akuma from an unknown number. Go figure; nothing much has changed.

"Hi, Adele. I was wondering if you could tell me the triplets' social security numbers?" he insisted.

"No, I'm not going to give you the triplets' social security numbers. If you were an active, responsible parent, you would already know them," I responded.

"I don't know if you remember from the divorce, but I was told by the Judge I get to claim the boys on my income tax return," he cajoled.

"Well, I don't know if you remember from the divorce, but the Judge said if you are a dollar off on child support, you receive nothing. Akuma, you are usually short $120 every month," I countered.

"Click."

I had hoped when he said his name on the call, a light bulb had gone off and he would have realized the importance of being in the triplets' lives full-time after Kingston's hospital stay. Nope. All he wanted was to use them as extra cash for his income tax return. He never cared about his children. It's always been about him and him alone.

Postpartum Injuries and More Health Concerns

My back issues were resolved in May of 2017 after doing physical therapy a couple of times a week and several sessions of dry needling in my lower back, hips and buttocks. The pain from my spinal block had finally healed. I could at last, after two and a half years, sit for more than thirty minutes at a time without extreme lower back pain.

In early September 2017, I found one doctor who was taking on new Medicaid patients. He was a podiatrist. He was able to start looking after my plantar fasciitis issues in both of my feet. It had been almost three years since the delivery of the triplets, and it was still so painful to walk or stand in place for long periods. I was now able to see a Medicaid provider to receive physical therapy, cupping, shoe inserts, and some very painful cortisone injections in both of my heels to help relieve the pain and pressure. I had an MRI test, which revealed my right foot had a plantar fascia rupture. I knew the pain I had wasn't imaginary. It was finally being recognized and treated.

In January of 2018, I continued to see my podiatrist for treatment. I saw my physical therapist twice a week regularly to help alleviate the pain. The discomfort stayed at a steadily high pain level most of the time. Even though the physical therapy was consistent, the relief was short-lived, and the pain always came back in full force.

In March of 2018, I landed wrong on my right foot, and with another MRI, two stress fractures were discovered in my right fifth metatarsal bone shaft and at the third metatarsal base. I had to use a walking boot for three to four weeks to heal my foot.

The Gift of Preschool

I had gone through so many medical issues since the birth of the triplets. It was a relief to know something wonderful was on the horizon in the fall of 2018. My mom and grandmother granted me the gift of sending the triplets to a Christian preschool twice a week to get a four-hour break from the grind of day-to-day operations as a single parent to multiples.

I was elated about this day, not only for each of them but for all that I had accomplished since they were born. The triplets had finally been potty-trained, and they could attend preschool.

> I wrote this on their first day of preschool:
>
> I remember the night before the triplets were born, I prayed for them as they were setting up the heart monitors to track their heartbeats.
>
> I remember very vividly listening to *Every Praise* by Hezekiah Walker throughout the night and trying to process everything this "Journey to Motherhood" would entail. After going through four and a half years of infertility, I was thrilled to embark on this task, as this dream of becoming a mother is something I always desired. I just never knew how challenging it would be.
>
> I have encountered many battles, heartbreaks, and circumstances many others do not know about.

The day of delivery I almost lost my life on the OR table; thanks to the doctors and the four blood transfusions, I survived and was able to recover without having a full hysterectomy. My recovery to becoming completely healthy after the triplets were born is still a work in progress. I've recovered from being wheelchair-bound a month after delivery for NICU visits, to two and a half years of severe pain in my lower back due to my spinal block during my C-section, a stress fracture in my knee in April of 2016, two stress fractures in my right foot in March of this year, and years of plantar fasciitis pain in both of my feet since carrying the triplets for 34 weeks.

I've gone through a divorce, and I've been raising the triplets on my own since they were newborns. I've been on my own, pulling all-nighters without the support of a loving and supportive partner for many years.

Yet, through every battle, heartbreak, and circumstance; God has been my fortress, my portion, and my hiding place. *Direct quote of lyrics from The Way by Pat Barrett.*

Many have given me the name "Wonder Woman," which humbles me and makes me realize that God has truly made me a warrior through this journey of motherhood that I continue to embark on.

I am forever grateful for the many individuals He has allowed to stand next to me, hold my precious babies in their hands, and help them develop and grow into precious little souls.

So, while today is a precious milestone for my beloved trio as they start preschool, it is also a milestone for me. I've literally prayed for this day for years. It may sound awkward praying for your kids to leave home and start their school day. However, after everything I've been through – this day is my reward.

My reward for the many battles, heartbreaks, and various circumstances. In each and every situation, there have been blessings, grace, faithfulness, and new mercies every morning.

So, this morning, we all got dressed, snapped a few photos for a memory keepsake, and got in the car.

> Instead of listening to *Every Praise* by Hezekiah Walker, we all listened to *The Way* by Pat Barrett.
>
> As I drove to school this morning, tears streamed down my face because I am **constantly** being reminded that God is my provider, my protector and the one I love. "As I continue this journey, every day is a new horizon and I'm set on Him. He met me here today with mercies that are new, all my fears and doubts, they can all come too because they will not stay long when I am here with you." (Lyrics by Pat Barrett from "*The Way*")

After their preschool-three school year and as they got ready for another gift of going to Pre-K, I was told the triplets should get tested for Gifted and Talented since they were thriving in their class.

"Good morning, Ms. Charles, thank you for bringing your children in to get tested today. Can I just pull you aside? I usually don't speak with parents after testing, but when I heard your story. I wanted to share a few things – first of all, I am absolutely amazed by you as a mom of triplets and having done this all on your own. Their academic level is way advanced. Secondly, I am finding their abilities intellectually mind-blowing. This is just incredible to see this in triplets.

Developmentally they are where they need to be at four and a half years old, but intellectually, absolutely mind-blowing. Their minds and way of thinking are way up there.

I've done hundreds if not thousands of these tests and I'm completely amazed by their intellectual abilities. As I've said, I don't speak with the parents following the tests, but I'm mind-blown by your abilities as a single parent of triplets. Just so amazed by the mom you are and who you are to these precious kids.

Your kids will eventually skip a grade; it's just a matter of what grade and how many they will skip.

Well done. Just amazing, Adele.

Please go sit in your car and pat yourself on your back. God has gifted you with these blessings, and you are doing a remarkable job."

"Thank you so much, that means so much to me," I graciously replied.

She had tears in her eyes and gave me a huge hug.

Dear Santa, I Want A Dad

An ongoing struggle the triplets had over the past couple of years always occurred at Christmas when Santa Claus arrived. It started at the age of three, and this year was no different. Since 2017, the triplets have asked Santa Claus for a dad for Christmas. It has been heart-wrenching as a mother to hear this. Most kids ask for toys, but my kids asked for a dad.

On December 22, 2018, at 6:16 a.m., I had a conversation with Reece.

"Mommy, do you have a husband yet?" Reece wondered.

"No, Reecy. Not yet," I felt saddened because I knew where this was going.

"Mommy, I want a daddy. How come I don't have a daddy?" he pondered.

"I know you do, bud. I don't know why you don't have a daddy," I answered.

"Mama, husbands can be daddies too," he encouraged.

"Yes, husbands can be daddies too. I know you want a daddy to cuddle with you and play with you and love you. Mama is praying for both, Reecy. I love you Reecy," I lovingly told him.

"I love you too, mama," Reece smiled back.

The last time Reece saw Akuma was on June 3, 2016.

Acceptance of New Medicaid Patient – 2019

In January 2019, I found a primary care doctor who was accepting new Medicaid patients. It had been at least three years of looking for a doctor to see me for a cold, wellness visits, and check-ups. I could finally see a doctor instead of having to wait until it was an emergency to visit the ED for my concerns.

In January, the twins, Reece and Kingston, had croup, and we were all very sick. For the most part, Scarlett missed what the boys had, but when I fell ill, it was so draining to tend to the children. I spent eleven long days and nights getting up night after night, taking care of the boys, and had to do nebulizer treatments with Kingston to prevent any further asthma attacks while he was sick. He ended up in the ED three days into the sickness with labored breathing.

I was living off of coffee to stay alert, and that was about it. I forgot to drink water and take care of myself while we were all down with this grueling sickness. It turns out, a diet of coffee while sick is not the best option. Around day four of the sickness, I developed symptoms of shortness of breath, my chest was tight, I couldn't stand up, and I was panting for breath.

My next-door neighbor took me to the ED while my mom stayed home to help with the triplets. Once I arrived, the doctor discovered I was severely dehydrated, and I was given three bags of IV fluids to help hydrate me.

"Ms. Charles, we are so glad you came in to get checked out. It sounds like you have a lot on your plate at home, raising triplets on your own," a nurse commented.

"Yeah, I do. When I get sick it seems to intensify greatly," I shared.

"Make sure to take care of yourself, too. Your vitals are all stable now. Your oxygen levels are back up. We can get the discharge set up. After your three IV bags, do you need to use the restroom?" she informed me.

"No, I don't," I said.

"Whoa, you were definitely dehydrated then. After three bags, and no?" she wondered again.

"No," I felt relieved and rehydrated.

"Maybe going forward, next time when the babies get sick or when you return home, ask people to text you to check and see if you've eaten or drank some water, okay?" she suggested.

"That sounds like a brilliant idea. I will do that now," I was grateful for the great care and understanding.

Releasing Bitterness and Unforgiveness

In March of 2019, I decided to work on healing my heartache after the divorce. My spiritual director and I parted ways as we were both moving in opposite directions.

I chose a Bible study by Lysa Terkeurst called: *It's Not Supposed to Be This Way: Finding Unexpected Strength When Disappointments Leave You Shattered*. It is beautifully written and helped me see every angle of everything I had felt and what God desires for me to see throughout all the hard times in my life.

The mornings the triplets were in preschool, I would pull up a chair at a local coffee shop to work on this study. I knew I needed healing, as the lack of help triggered me in negative ways. I carried so much weight and so much baggage. I had played both parenting roles since the day they were born. It was more than I could bear most days. I desired to find wholeness, spiritual, mental, and emotional healing from everything I went through.

Because when everything hit the fan, the children were only five months old, and the focus was on them and their well-being. I had to do so much for them that I didn't second guess a thing, nor did I start thinking of myself. It was mind over matter at that time – I was in survival mode and had no time to think about the divorce or how I was being treated. The memories of the hurt and abuse were always there, but to process the hurt, I didn't have time to do this with three preemies.

I recall one morning in this study listening to music in my headphones as I began to weep. It was then that I began to declare forgiveness over Akuma's shortcomings. I spent a significant amount of time reflecting and spending a great deal of time in solitude. I was able to release and begin to process the hurt after deep-diving into this study.

Tears streamed down my face as the bitterness and hurt left my heart, which had kept me a slave to all the brokenness. I prayed over all the sadness and disappointment I felt after going through IVF only to be abandoned and rejected months later. It was a good step toward my healing. I found myself having to forgive him often, as there were so many disappointments since October of 2014. I was able to find some peace from my past, forgive Akuma for his actions, let go of strongholds, and embrace my grit.

Chained By Pain

By August of 2019, I continued to see my podiatrist for checkups as I had increased my physical therapy appointments and began different strategies to help alleviate the agony of my bilateral plantar fasciitis. I was doing everything I had done before and could only get a total of three cortisone injections in each of my heels. Therefore, I started a new treatment of dry needling along with electro-stimulation during my sessions.

I began to think this would never heal as it was unbearable for me. I had a conversation with God in my thoughts:

God, this is debilitating. I can't run or work out like I want. I can't get rid of this baby weight I still struggle to lose. God, I'm at a point where if none of these treatments work, I am willing to amputate my feet to not deal with this excruciating pain anymore. I am so desperate. Please, God. Heal my feet.

A Body Torn and Rebuilt

By December 2019, I began feeling more discomfort in my abdomen when sitting up and lying down. I was given a referral from my new primary care doctor to see a specialist who focused on inguinal hernia, ventral hernia, and other conditions at varying frequencies, care, and surgery.

Before Christmas, I scheduled an appointment with this specialist to be examined. The doctor performed a physical examination first, and then I had a scheduled CT scan done the day after Christmas.

In early January of 2020, the CT scan showed I had an incarcerated ventral hernia in the front of my abdominal wall where some of my intestines had pushed through, probably from carrying the triplets. A weakness in my abdominal muscles became trapped, hence incarcerated, in that opening. It couldn't be pushed back in without having surgery. It was important to treat this as soon as possible, so it wouldn't become a strangulated hernia, which is a surgical emergency, and potentially lead to necrosis, a serious infection.

I also had two epigastric hernias around the abdominal wall between the belly button, (umbilicus) and the lower end of the breastbone (sternum), along the midline.

The CT scan also revealed significant, tremendous, and advancing diastasis recti, as well as destruction of my abdominal wall structure from previously carrying triplets. The diastasis recti was so severe it was considered a complete separation, where the gap was over seven centimeters wide, or the equivalent of four fingers or more. My midline was almost entirely stretched open; my fascia was extremely thin in areas or absent in spots. If the diastasis recti wasn't repaired as soon as possible. I might develop more hernias than I had and require further surgeries down the road.

I was scheduled to have a total of three surgeries: hernia repair, diastasis recti repair, and by choice, an abdominoplasty. I scheduled everything at once because I couldn't imagine having to go under the knife again.

The last time I was in the OR was during my traumatic delivery; the fear and anxiety brought so much terror I experienced repetitive panic and anxiety attacks leading up to the surgery scheduled at the end of February 2020.

For the past two years, I had been on meds for severe anxiety, so I found it comforting knowing I could take something to ease my deepest concern – dying on the operating table. What may have looked like a regular procedure for the surgeons was my next trepidation, and I began to think I was going to die.

As I sat in the pre-operative room going over the surgery and what to expect, feelings of anxiety washed over me. It was bone-deep, marrow-shaking trepidation that lived in my chest like a coiled snake.

The last time I lay on an operating table, I had felt the world slip away in a haze of sterile lights and cold metal, only to be dragged back from the edge by frantic voices and the prickling burn of oxygen flooding my lungs and blood being squeezed through an IV pressure bag bringing my nearly lifeless body back to life.

Now, even the thought of surgery again made my stomach seize and my throat tighten as if the air itself might betray me. Every smell of antiseptic turned my skin clammy. Every glimpse of a hospital corridor made my pulse drum in my ears.

It wasn't just the memory of trauma – it was the memory of helplessness, of floating in a void where I could never speak nor fight for my life. The idea of surrendering my body to anesthesia felt like inviting death back into the room, politely asking it to stay at my bedside. The question lingered like the scent of perfume in a fragrance shop – "What if I don't wake up from this?"

"Are you sure this will go, okay?" I asked while my body trembled.

"Yes, I can assure you, you will do fine," the surgeon answered.

The surgery was supposed to take over eight hours to complete; it was completed in about four and a half hours. Everything went smoothly. I stayed in the hospital a couple of nights, more so for my sake and worries, in case there were complications and because I had very active five-year-old triplets at home.

I had help lined up for the first month post-op so I could recover after being told to be on bedrest for at least four weeks. I wanted to make sure I had ample time to recover from major abdominal surgery because after the C-section I was thrown through the trenches of having to do everything on my own. I was grateful my triplets were five years old and not newborn preemies this go around.

The recovery from these three surgeries was much more painful, and it seemed more difficult to recover from. I had an inner scar from my chest cavity down to my pubic bone to repair the hernias and my diastasis recti, and an outer scar that crossed at my panty line from the furthest side of my left hip all the way to my right hip from the abdominoplasty.

God's Glory is Evident

I knew after this triple surgery how much of a miracle had occurred in my life during my C-section. I think about the blood loss – 66.7% blood volume lost, equivalent to three liters of blood lost, Hemorrhagic Shock – all of it. A miracle from God that I overcame all of this!

God knew I needed to be there for my precious babies. He allowed me to live to be here for them and to raise them. I knew he had a purpose for my life. Somehow, someway, God would use everything I have gone through for His glory.

I noticed God working in my life after the surgery in 2020 as well. My dad and I had a very rocky start from my early childhood, through adolescence, and into my adult life. We hadn't spoken for almost twelve years and then, God brought him back into my life when I was pregnant with the triplets.

Our relationship began during my pregnancy and has grown since the birth of my triplets. God touched my dad's heart after my triple surgery when I needed some help getting around post-op. He took me to a follow-up post-op appointment, took me grocery shopping, and bought a few things I needed for recovery and things for my kids. These were all things he had not done before, and it brought me to tears.

I had been on bed rest for about a month when my dad reached out to me and mentioned a movie he saw and wanted me to watch.

"Hey Del, it's Dad. I was just calling to check on you and see how you were," he disclosed.

"Hi Dad, I'm making good progress. Still taking it easy, watching a lot of shows and movies. Everything has slowed down greatly. The kids are staying home because of all the COVID stuff going on. But I'm used to being at home with them most days. It's not very different for us," I shared.

"Well, if you are watching TV, have you ever seen '*I Can Only Imagine*'?" he asked.

"I haven't seen the movie, but I've listened to the song. It's a good song," I said.

"If you have time, watch it. It was a great movie," he commented.

Later that evening, I found the movie on Prime Video and watched it. I ended up crying throughout the whole movie. It reminded me of my own broken relationship I had with my dad all those years ago.

The behaviors he had displayed over the past couple of months were something I had never seen before, nothing I had ever seen in my entire life. It was so beautiful.

What I gathered from the movie was he was the dad and I was the son. In my heart, I felt it was his way of saying sorry for all the hurt he caused in my life all those years ago. Tears fell from my cheeks. I loved this new version of him. My father began to look after me, care for me, and took great pride in being there for my triplets.

Every day with my dad has been better than the last. His heart has softened, and God continues to work things out for good for those who love him.

Miracle Worker

In late spring of 2020, I experienced yet another huge miracle. I believe it had something to do with being on bed rest, healing properly, taking it easy, having my abdominal wall reconnected again to make me feel whole, along with the abdominoplasty and a complete answer to prayer – my bilateral severe plantar fasciitis pain had completely healed!

Where once I had walked around like a wounded pirate for almost six years – hobbling, grimacing, and uttering words until my breath – one glorious morning I swung my legs off my bed, planted my feet on the floor, and…nothing.

No stabbing pain. No searing burn. Just the quiet, blissful hum of normalcy.

I wasn't sure if this was a false hope that would soon disappear like my moments of relief after a session at physical therapy. I would often stand suspiciously, like someone testing ice on a frozen pond. I took a step. Then another. Then, because life is short, I ran, twirled, and strutted to the kitchen to grab a spoon, turned on my favorite playlist, and danced until I couldn't anymore, and my feet never hurt while I pranced around singing to my couch and my dining room table.

My plantar fasciitis was gone, and so was the fear of standing and walking around. I decided to mark this newfound freedom with a jog as a family to the park. I remember this day vividly.

On June 20, 2020, I wanted to make sure this was a day to remember. I wrote this down in my journal.

> Team Charles
>
> Day 1 – The significance of today marks a new era for the Charles Family. I've personally waited close to six years for this day. I went through several years of infertility and luckily only had to complete one IVF cycle to create my family. During the prep

period of IVF, I was told not to work up a sweat per protocol, so running was out.

During my high-risk pregnancy of carrying multiples, running was out.

Upon delivery, which I consider the most traumatic experience of my life, my doctors, after several appointments and medical advice told me to not work out for at least one year. Running was out.

After completing physical therapy, cortisone injections, shoe inserts, medical opinions, MRI's, dry needling, leg splints, being prayed over, and for the most part of five plus years of not being able to walk well, running was out.

This past February, I needed to have three surgeries due to three hernias and a 3-inch separation from my abdominal wall from my chest cavity down to my pubic bone. I had hopes of being able to resolve some issues and if not, receive complete healing over my feet issues I had from carrying three beautiful souls. I had hopes of returning to this new era.

Recovering properly from these surgeries was a top priority for me. Thank God I wasn't tending to preemies this time around. This was more difficult to heal from, which is surprising to me to this day.

I should have died when I delivered the triplets, yet I'm still here. #Godswarrior

The surgeries I had in February put me back for over six weeks. I had helped lined up for a whole month; however social distancing took over and my mom was left tending to my family solo.

Prayer works. God gets the glory.

Just this past Tuesday, I completed my three-month post-op.

I have been cleared to return to normal life and any exercise I want.

Today, my tribe jogged with me.

Running is back! I'm back!

COVID and Homeschooling

My dreams of returning to work were short-lived because of the COVID pandemic. Everything remained closed for several months even though the triplets were going to be kindergarteners in the fall of 2020.

Over the summer, several of my former colleagues and friends from the Virgin Islands encouraged me to homeschool. I was completely against it at first because I was around the kids **all** the **time** and craved adult time. I wanted to work outside of the house, but when the lockdowns were imposed, I didn't have a choice.

I tested the idea of homeschooling in July and discovered how much I loved it.

Our first homeschooling year was set to start mid-August.

Once school started, the triplets flew through the kindergarten curriculum. I bought a math workbook online that I thought would take four months to complete; however, it was completed in one month. Afterward, I purchased a first-second grade math workbook in mid-September thinking it would last through the new year, and it was completed by November. The triplets knew everything a kindergartener should know and more within three months, so I decided to graduate them from kindergarten, and I began teaching first grade in January. Homeschooling the triplets was our greatest and most rewarding investment as a family.

Because COVID was such a scary time for so many, I continued to choose to homeschool because I felt called to do it. Kingston had so many emergency department visits in the past, and being the only caretaker of my family, I opted to avoid the fear of leaving someone behind if any of my kids got the virus because so many family members were not allowed to leave the hospital once someone tested positive.

Many family members were left behind and not even allowed to visit a sick loved one. I never wanted that lifestyle for my kids, let alone subject them to wearing masks 24/7 and being isolated from others.

Where God Shows Up

Over the course of my life since becoming the "Triplet Mama," I have begun to keep a journal on my phone under my notes app to track all of God's goodness in my life.

I use this note section titled, "List Where God Has Shown Up," as a constant reminder for me when I feel discouraged along my journey. It's a note I fall back on, especially when it's been difficult living in the unknown from year to year. Yet, it blesses me every time because I can see God's goodness all throughout my life as a mother.

These are some of the ways God has shown up in my journey:

- Set aside versus being set apart for a greater purpose

- AMH score from .9 to .7 and it jumped up to 2.1
- God tells me, "The reason this child is taking so long to come to be is because I will be glorified in it.
- IVF works the first time
- My chances of getting pregnant with one were a 65% chance, with a 40% chance of having twins, and a 0.6% chance of having triplets
- I carried my completely healthy triplets to 34 weeks and one day
- I was never on bed rest even though my pregnancy was considered extremely high risk
- My triplets never showed signs of developmental delays even though they were six weeks early
- Their language development exploded at 18 months
- Meals were cooked and delivered throughout the first seven months
- Volunteers provided two years of help to care for and love the triplets free of charge
- We never had to buy diapers for up to eight months
- Triplets were tested for gifted and talented programs

The list is ongoing, and I love looking back to see the different ways God has always had my best interests at heart and in mind. My Lord, Jesus, has looked after and protected the triplets all along.

El Roi - The God Who Sees Me

There are moments in our life when we feel invisible to the world – abandoned, alone, isolated. Know that you have not escaped God's notice. He sees you right where you are.

I wrote these exact words on a chalkboard in my kitchen after attending a Mothers of Preschoolers meeting, before my divorce. The words, "El Roi – The God Who Sees Me" are still on my chalkboard to this day. It's another reminder for me to remember that God knows – he knows when I struggle, he knows when I hurt and he knows how tough this journey has been as a single parent. I may be single to the world around me, but I'm never alone.

All of our stories matter to God. He guides us through the darkness if we are willing to fall to our knees and see Him through. The more we depend on Jesus, the more we will see God's handiwork in our lives.

Our prayers for our young sons matter because one day these boys will grow up to be men. I want my sons, Reece and Kingston, to have a kingdom impact on the world around them. I desire for my sons to lead as Godly men in a world where many men fall short of their abilities to lead, provide and protect.

I am reminded all the time that God will be glorified through the birth of my children, and I was never set aside but set apart from a greater purpose – to bring the lost back to him, to bring His children home.

The Lord Jesus is patiently waiting for us to turn to Him and Him alone. For years I couldn't see beyond the heartache, yet Jesus waited for me. I wrote this poem after reading my Bible one afternoon. I had read through 2 Peter 3:9 and within ten minutes, God put these word on my heart.

He Waited for Me

A beautiful aspect of the gospel - God is so patient with us.

Lord, Jesus,
Thank you for being patient with my brokenness.
For my shortcomings
My unforgiveness
My habitual sins
My unbelief

There has been so much emptiness
Throughout the years
Feelings of unworthiness
Shame
Guilt
Pain
Rejection
Abandonment

So many failed relationships

Friendships
A marriage

Lies told
Promises unkept
Vows disregarded

A feeling of being so lost
Wondering if you were real
O me of little faith

Afraid to be seen
In such a heartless and cold world
Being judged by the traumas I've faced
I often wondered
Why would you choose me?
Why did you choose to die for me?

Rescue me
Search after me in all of my brokenness
You never stopped looking for me
I found you in worship
Prayer
Earthly angels
Rare occurrences

And you were patient with me
You were so patient with me.

I am astounded by your patience.

I was so thirsty to be seen and heard
Validated and understood

Even in my unhealthy longing and looking in every direction, but yours…

You waited for me.

This world has turned upside down
So much hurt
Confusion
Hopelessness rises around me

Yet, in this moment
You surround me
Cover me
Anoint my spirit

And I am in awe of your patience towards me.

I see you
I see you so clearly now
The narrow path
Is the path I seek

To be near to you

I long only for your embrace

The holy scriptures I cling to
You are my lifeline
My only hope

Your patience towards me
In all this time
Years of so much trauma
Pulling away
Running back
Walking away
Weeping out your name
Falling to my knees
Repenting
Seeking forgiveness
Being washed clean

You never thought twice
Dying for me on that cross that day

You cried out my name and prayed for me to return home
You waited so patiently

And when I realized fully who you were
What you had done
What you continue to do
And what I mean to you

I dropped the baggage
The pain
The brokenness
The weight of all the years
And ran into your open arms

You held me
With your own scarred hands
You took all the weight I carried and held

And made me new
You called me by name
I knew I would be forever yours

Jesus, thank you for loving me so much
That you would wait for me
To know who I am in you

I love you, your beloved daughter
- Adele

The Price of Neglect

In the fall of 2022, Akuma stopped making child support payments. In August, I received $122.48, and through the end of the year, nothing. I began having more anxiety about how to support the triplets, continue paying my bills, and buy groceries with inflation on the rise.

His lack of support caused horrible anxiety and I was left to figure it all out, as usual. I always thought, ***"Geez, I do it all****. The least Akuma could do is pay his damn child support."*

After dealing with the Child Support system for years, I learned no one can file or reach out to Child Support Services until a full thirty days of no support has passed. As soon as the thirty days passed, I sent my next email to my caseworker, letting her know I hadn't received anything but $122.48 since August.

By December of 2022, it was my birthday and my sister sent me this text:

Aster: Happy, happy birthday, sis! I hope you know how very loved, admired and celebrated you are! You inspire me daily with your brilliance, courage, resilience, and fortitude! You are the strongest woman I know and such an incredible light for Christ! I hope this next year brings great blessings and abundance for you and that God fulfills the deepest longings of your heart! I hope you have a wonderful day and we need to schedule a time to grab lunch and celebrate both our birthdays now!

I needed some encouragement and in such a big way. To hear this from my sister made me feel loved, celebrated, and appreciated for all I do. Aster has always considered me as,

"Wonder Woman." Well, Wonder Woman was exhausted from carrying the load she carries. I am so tired of being resilient.

Can I just exhale for once? Why such a heavy load, God? What purpose is there in all of this?

I reached out to my caseworker again in January of 2023 and she could not locate an income source of his, so they couldn't do anything. The waiting game of the system to play catch up with his lack is when it would supposedly trigger reinforcement. No reinforcement for five plus months sounded like a broken system.

How could he be working and there be no garnished wages? Who is at fault here? The system? Akuma's place of employment? Akuma? It angered me deeply.

Akuma continued to not pay child support up through February of 2023. I had had enough with his continued lack.

I already had been in contact with a lawyer and was ready to move forward with some legal services to get the child support owed to me to take care of the triplets' basic needs.

Akuma could care less about their basic needs – food? Clothing? Shelter? Health care? Education? Nothing mattered to him, but himself.

The only issue that needed to be resolved was where to find Akuma. I never had a way to communicate with him since March of 2016. I hadn't heard from him since April of

2017, when he had asked about getting the kids' SSNs rather than asking about how his kids were doing.

I began doing random internet searches searching for his name and just like the detective work I used before, I found where Akuma worked via the internet with a search of an image, along with his name and the city he lived in. I found him because I recognized a picture he took from another dating website, where once again, he lied about his name and his age. He went from Akuma, to Dennis1806, to Anwir and from age 59, to 34 to 44. BINGO!

By early March of 2023, the ball dropped and things were being organized by my lawyer's firm to file several motions to get this case going. The two major motions I cared most about were the Motion to Modify Child Support and the Motion and Affidavit of Criminal Contempt.

Somehow, I began receiving various child support payments throughout the month of March. Every year, since our divorce, Akuma's income tax return has always been intercepted because of his lack and inconsistent child support payments.

The firm now had been able to confirm Akuma's workplace, yet through various skip traces could not find his home address. They wanted to serve him the papers there; however, it was unknown. They had searched for the whole month of March, but to no avail they could not locate his home address.

I asked him to be served at his workplace. He was served on April 6, 2023.

Work Woes, More Miracles and Skin Cancer

At the end of March 2023, another health scare arose along with losing my only client I had that year. I always followed the requirements by the state to continue my food stamps and Medicaid. The one requirement needed to maintain my benefits was to be working a minimum of twenty hours a week. Homeschooling didn't count for whatever reason, and the thought of losing my only source of income brought more anxiety into my world.

Because I did it all, all of the responsibilities fell into my lap. I provided food and nutrition for my children. I kept them in a safe and clean home environment. I managed the household chores – laundry, cleaning, dishes. I paid the bills and managed the household budget. I scheduled and attended all the appointments – medical and activities. I planned every school lesson for years, as I continued to homeschool. I graded tests. I chose every school year's curriculum. I taught them. I couldn't afford childcare, even if I worked a full-time job, so I was their full-time nanny. I met all of their emotional needs – comfort when sick or injured, encouragement when learning new things or when they were sad – love and lots of it. I helped with homework. I set rules, boundaries and discipline. I encouraged healthy habits – exercise, play, hygiene, and sleep routines. I planned activities and supervised all of them. I took them to doctor and dentist appointments. I taught them safety skills. I taught them values, manners and life skills. I supported their hobbies, talents and personal growth. I prepared the triplets for life and future responsibilities. I taught them about Jesus and the importance of having a relationship with him. I helped maintain their own physical and mental health. I juggled running my business while homeschooling and being a full-time mom. I was their emotional anchor and role model for resilience.

Yet according to the state of Colorado, if I wasn't working at least twenty hours a week, I wasn't doing enough, and the thought of losing my food stamps and Medicaid threw me into the fire of being triggered. **I AM NOT ENOUGH.** If only, I could make more money. If only…

At the same time as losing my only client, I was diagnosed with basal cell carcinoma on my forehead near my hairline and was scheduled to have surgery. In addition, a squamous cell carcinoma on my right cheek below my eye needed to be treated with topical chemotherapy cream.

It was too much to handle at one time, so I reached out to a team member on my greeting team at church. I explained what was happening and how I began praying for another job.

Then something happened: another miracle!

My greeting leader reached out to his small group from church, and they concocted a plan. Within one day of losing my only client, I had a new job working for a company owned by one of his small group attendees. It's a company with a team of engineers and brilliant minds who develop technological superiority in smart autonomous systems. It was supposed to be a temporary gig working part-time, but ten months later, I was promoted, and I've been working there ever since. The people I work with have continued to bless my life and the life of my family.

I had basal cell carcinoma removed using local anesthesia after going to stage two of the Mohs surgery. I had a 1.2 x 1cm tumor removed from my upper forehead. I literally had a hole in my head after stage two, I turned white from just looking at it. After the removal, I had twenty-eight stitches placed on my forehead to close the gaping hole in my forehead. Following the surgery, I experienced the most severe headaches I've ever had in my life for several days.

Court Cases 2023

Our hearing for the modification of child support was scheduled and after a thorough discussion with Child Support Services, known as CSS, and the court the determination was made to increase my child support by $419.00.

From the transcripts I purchased from court and through his testimony, Akuma was not planning on being present for his children going forward, which confused me a great deal on the fact that we paid extraordinary costs to complete an IVF cycle. He said several unpleasant things during our hearings and claimed some unbelievable reasons as to why he couldn't be an active parent to his own flesh and blood. All to which, he never provided documented proof or evidence of.

In my opinion, during the criminal contempt case, the court system placed more weight on his spoken words than on his actual actions, despite the glaring absence of documented proof to support his claims. Time and again, he stood before the Judge empty-handed: no records, no receipts, no credible evidence. Yet, his assertions were taken at face value.

Meanwhile, I had carefully gathered and submitted documentation, complete with receipts and records, that clearly demonstrated the truth.

Still, the court dismissed four of the five criminal charges, absolving him of responsibility when the evidence should have pointed to guilt.

If justice truly requires that criminals be proven guilty beyond a reasonable doubt, then this case revealed a troubling reality – in that courtroom, words seemed to carry more weight than evidence, despite years of contempt and neglect. There was a measly consequence of a $100 fine to the court for failing to pay child support consistently or on time for over eight years. Every other court order was neglected completely due to his disregard and had no consequence, no accountability, and no punishment, even though he was found guilty of punitive contempt.

Exhausted

I wrote this shortly after the devastating blow at the sentencing hearing:

I hold all the responsibility.
I bear the guilt of marrying such a selfish fool.
I feel I have let my children down.
I married someone who is evil, selfish, narcissistic, abusive, a deadbeat sperm donor, who has only cared about his own selfish needs and no one else's.
He cannot see what a child goes through, nor has he cared about their basic needs: food, clean water, shelter, or clothing.
He is incapable of love.
He is someone who prides himself on neglecting others, neglecting responsibility, neglecting his own flesh and blood.

He is someone who finds joy in abandoning his family, his former two wives with broken hearts and five children who know nothing of what a father is.
He speaks words with no action.
His words are empty.
His actions – none.

Thank you for showing me I deserve more.
Thank God, he rescued me from your destruction.
Thank you for allowing me to see who you really are after I gave birth.
Thank you for leaving, so your traits of abusive behavior never affected Reece, Kingston, and Scarlett.
Thank you for showing me what a grown boy looks and acts like:
He has excuses.
He lies.
He lacks character.
He lacks integrity.
He lacks love.
He lacks responsibility.
He is a coward.
He is a follower.
He confuses you.
He rarely communicates with you.
He ignores your needs.
He uses you.

He isn't accountable.
He speaks words of death.
He is abusive.
Uncommitted.
I know now what I will never accept in my life. Thank you for leaving me alone.

I went through so much heartache. So many physical setbacks. I fought through PTSD, trauma after trauma, only to rise above the fires you set around me and within me. You left me in ashes.
But guess what - - every fire you started and waited for me to die and suffer - - Jesus was standing in the fire with me.
He picked me up when you pushed me down.
He held my hand when you left.
He came to every doctor appointment, physical therapy appointment, surgery, and reminded me who I am.

I am an overcomer.
A survivor of domestic violence.
I am a strong person.
I am a phenomenal mom of triplets.
I am an amazing teacher.
I can multi-task and support my kids regardless of what I went through.
Jesus was right there.
In every fire.
He was there.

The Deadbeat Diaries

Akuma complied with all child support orders up through June 2024, but nothing else – no communication, no financial information, no payment of uninsured health-related costs, no calls, nothing. He was doing what he always did best: absolutely nothing. I made sure to document all of it – the lack of responses to every text and email I sent him. He was always in contempt.

He paid child support up through June until I received a call from a debt collector calling inquiring about his whereabouts on June 17, 2024.

I spoke with the debt collector for about thirty minutes, providing her with the information she needed to find him. After all, I knew how she felt. I searched for years, only to be let down by the court system and child support services.

I gave her the information she needed and thought nothing more about it until I received a letter from CSS around early July 2024 about Akuma wanting to lower it when we just changed about a year ago.

On July 30th, there was a hearing scheduled with CSS, Akuma, and me. He didn't want to communicate with me about his requests, yet CSS explained that he couldn't afford to pay child support because he was attending appointments for his terminal disease several days a week and I was told he would be applying for disability.

This, of course, was news to me as he never communicates with me about anything. I shared my frustration with CSS, and she understood my hindrance and confusion. I asked her if there was any evidence sent in, and she said there was a little bit that she would forward to me.

I began to look through all the evidence Akuma sent into CSS. He never cared to email, text, or mail it to me. I received it via email from CSS. I received a medical document contradicting a terminal disease he claimed he had several times under oath just a month after our court cases in 2023. There is no way someone with this condition, would suddenly not have this disease within one month of it being terminal, let alone after claiming under oath of seeing three to four doctors at a time as well as not having any prior documentation of terminal disease or diagnosis.

This was the only document related to his apparent illness. No paperwork showing evidence of disease, diagnoses, when his appointments were – nothing. I found this odd because he had a new claim of attending several appointments a week for his new disease for over the course of six months and there was only one document sent in as "proof".

His new document gave him a new ethnicity, said that he was now fluent in the English language and spoke an additional language of Spanish, even though in our divorce proceedings he only spoke Spanish and a little bit of English.

CSS explained to both of us there needed to be a court hearing to discuss the request to modify child support given by Akuma.

I was furious to have to think about going to court again.

For what?

There was no justice when I was there.

I lost all trust in the system after what occurred, yet I also knew I wouldn't go down without a fight. This time, I would fight this fight myself.

After seeing my lawyer file all but twenty-five exhibits from the plethora of evidence I sent in, for seven years of my arduous journey – I knew my story the best. I am incredibly organized, and I make quite a good investigator, detective, and soon-to- be, my own paralegal.

Throughout the month of August, my mom, dad, brothers, and sister all received calls from various debt collectors looking for Akuma. His actions of contempt carried over into his own life, not just mine.

Pro Se and Tenacious

In August, I spent the whole month doing the following: printing evidence, paying for court transcripts, organizing files, scanning my documents, organizing exhibits, adding numbered tabs, organizing notebooks, writing a table of contents, researching the local courts on how to write and file my own affidavits, motions, and exhibit lists, and I wrote a lengthy letter to the court.

I filed 160 exhibits with the court, CSS, and Akuma on August 29, 2024.

Then I waited…

I waited some more…

Akuma was supposed to set up mediation between the two of us within fourteen days of August 29, by September 12, 2024. He never called or reached out to me to set it up. The case should have been dismissed, but the Judge gave him an extension to have it completed by October 30, 2024. Once again, in Akuma fashion, the extension was granted, and he never set up the mediation. The case should have been dismissed twice because he never followed the court order to establish mediation. All these chances and opportunities for the respondent to comply, and every order denied on his behalf.

I sent emails to Riven, my caseworker at CSS, multiple times – no child support in July, August, September ($400.00), no child support in October, or November.

I was tired of the lack of Akuma, the Court, and CSS. Child Support Services should change their name to Deadbeat Parent Services, because they did nothing for my children.

I had enough.

I had a conversation with Jesus, my Lord and Savior, and told him I couldn't do this anymore. This man and this system had let me down for so many years. I struggled year after year, being triggered by the lack. I held so much inside. I would go for months to church and weep at every Sunday service.

Being a single mom to triplets has been so challenging. Living in the unknown month after month, year after year, was taking a toll on me in every way.

After my conversation, I heard Jesus tell me – file for contempt one more time, and when you do, be done with all of this.

The Funeral – My Last Cry for Justice

I filed for contempt in December 2024, and submitted a total of 170 exhibits, along with 24 handwritten witness statements for court. I filed for all the same charges as before. Once I filed for contempt, the court finally took me seriously. I was given an order to issue a citation to show cause on December 16, 2024. I asked the sheriff's office to serve him, yet the sheriff's office couldn't locate him.

I requested to have an alias citation to show cause for the contempt citation after the settlement conference in January 2025, regarding Akuma's petition to modify child support – where he was once again, a no show.

He should've been held in contempt of court for never setting up mediation months in a row from August to October, for ignoring and not following orders of the court. But hey, why bother, right? The courts seem to support deadbeats and criminals.

Akuma's motion was withdrawn by CSS, since he never appeared in court. He never sent in any evidence of terminal disease, anything about him being on disability, or anything to the court since he made his request in July 2024.

I have to believe it was all a lie as well. I think over the years he was learning how to be a criminal and how to get out of his court-ordered obligations, and now, attempted to get out of child support completely.

I was given the alias citation to show cause, for a hearing scheduled in February 2025, along with an additional ten days to find him. This time I used a private investigator.

The P.I. searched three national databases, made at least twenty different attempts to serve him at his address he shared in court in 2023, and discovered Akuma has been busy creating various aliases – at least three different names with the same SSN.

To this day, Akuma is still a fugitive.

I attempted to file various motions in February 2025: to enforce court orders along with an additional letter to the court, a re-issuance of the alias citation, a verified entry of support judgment, an additional motion and affidavit of contempt requesting the court to charge Akuma with a criminal misdemeanor and potential felony offense subject to federal prosecution in accordance with Section 228, Title 18; a request to deny him of a passport, a request for discovery of Akuma's various bank accounts, credit cards, medical records, termination letter from past employment, and to place liens on all of his accounts. I requested full custody of my children and asked the court to give sole guardianship to my brother in case something would happen to me.

At the hearing in late February, the Judge denied everything I requested and told me, "Well, the child support order remains."

I was told the district court couldn't charge a misdemeanor or felony without a federal case, even though it was supposed to be handled at the state and local level first.

The Judge told me I needed to file motions with the court to get full custody and that sole guardianship wasn't an issue to be handled now.

So, tell me...what would be the point of filing motions again when the sheriff's office cannot find him, a private investigator cannot locate him, the court doesn't hold him in contempt, CSS doesn't do anything – and you want me to file motions knowing it will go nowhere.

Justice was never found.

Breakthrough

There was a plethora of evidence stacked against him, and because he is a fugitive, he cannot be formally charged. Nor will I see the desired kind of justice on this side of heaven.

So many friends and family members had prayed for me for years, since I became pregnant with the triplets, postpartum, and in the court cases that occurred in 2023, 2024, and 2025.

As God began to speak with me during these disastrous court cases, he told me this:

I am chosen, not forsaken.
I am not abandoned; I am adopted by the Most High and Holy God.
I am not a widow.
I am officially on the guest list of the wedding banquet of Christ Jesus.
My children are not orphans; they are heirs to King Jesus.
He loves me; he brings me new life every day
through his promises of yes and amen.
He pulls me out of the darkness and brings me into his light.

What Satan meant for evil – when he came to steal, kill, and destroy –

BUT GOD…

He turns it around for good.
He lavishly releases blessings and treasures for his people.
God is the foundation of life.
He is the only source of my hope.
He brings life, being Jehovah Rapha, Jehovah Nissi, Jehovah Jireh.
Jesus is majestic, omnipotent, and omnipresent.
His name is marvelous.
He surpasses them all.
He is El Roi and my perfect peace.
He is my shalom, my lifeboat.
He is my savior and our perfect creator.

He welcomes my triplets and me into his gift of eternal life.
After all these trials, sorrows, and heartaches, I will come forth as GOLD.
He has counted all my tears; he holds them in his hands and in his heart.
Nothing is wasted. Nothing is lacking.
Nothing is broken. Nothing is missing.
Nothing is damaged.
I declare Dabar Shalom over my family,
my finances, my physical body, my mental health.
I am covered from head to toe in the blood of the lamb.

God's Fingerprints and Promises

"Don't be afraid. Stand firm and watch God do his work of salvation for you today. Take a good look at the Egyptians today for you're never going to see them again."

- Exodus 14:13 The Message Translation

"God answered Moses, "So, do you think I can't take care of you? You'll see soon enough."
- Numbers 11:23a The Message Translation

Jesus spoke to me throughout the various series of traumas I experienced in my life. So, when Jesus asked me to surrender after filing for contempt on December 2, 2024, he continued to speak to me through his holy and written word – the Holy Bible.

The more I read his holy book, the more I realized his handprints were woven throughout my life, particularly since I became a mom to triplets.

Where I once thought I was rejected and abandoned – Jesus taught me I was protected and set apart.

Jesus spoke to me on the morning of August 4, 2024, when I was preparing for court and shared these verses with me. He woke me up at 6:08 a.m. and asked me to read these scriptures in this order:

"Away from me, all you who do evil, for the Lord has heard my weeping."

Psalms 6:8 NIV

"Then I heard the voice of the Lord saying, "Whom shall I send? And who will go for us?" And I said, "Here I am, send me!"

Isaiah 6:8 NIV

"But Noah found favor in the eyes of the Lord."

Genesis 6:8 NIV

"He sent them a prophet, who said, "The God of Israel, says: I brought you up out of Egypt, out of the land of slavery."

Judges 6:8 NIV

"I sent him this reply: Nothing like what you are saying is happening; you are just making it up in your head."

Nehemiah 6:8 NIV

"Do not be like them, for your Father knows what you need before you ask him."

Matthew 6:8 NIV

Jesus told me I was being released from Akuma's evil ways. He told me my story would be used for God's glory. I would find favor in God's eyes. I was leaving the land of slavery and would soon walk into the land of promise he set out for me. Jesus reassured me Akuma was a liar and made everything up. God reminded me of my integrity and to surrender everything to Him. Knowing He is Jehovah Jireh – the God who provides, and El Roi – the God who sees me.

The following day I was polishing this silver platter my late grandmother and best friend, Ya Ya, left to me, and I wrote this excerpt while I worked out the tarnishes.

The Thought of Polishing Silver

Dirty, filthy, tarnished from years of neglect without the knowledge or existence of Christ in our lives.

The back represents experiences in our lives that left stains, scars, and memories of hurts, tragedies, and traumas we've left in our hearts. Some of these are hidden from view of others in fear of judgement, in fear of being seen.

See, God is waiting for us to acknowledge and encounter him in the most heartfelt ways so he can begin the process of refining what we hide. He sees the deepest hurt, the stains, the hardened heart.

He can hardly wait for us to run to him, to seek him, to return to him, and learn how to follow him daily.

Jesus is the only one who can refine us, make us clean, and wash us new. He wants to give you a soft heart and wipe the years of neglect away.

And the scars and stains that remain, you ask?

He uses those to bless others. God can make broken into beautiful.

God can take the stains and utilize them for his glory.

Those scars, Jesus has those scars too.

He can turn what was meant for bad and turn it around for good.

Sometimes we only want Jesus when life is good. Sometimes we only want Jesus when life is bad.

Jesus wants us daily - when we cry, when we're grieving, when we celebrate, when we are filled with laughter. He wants us.

We all have a choice in this life. We can choose Him day after day in all things, or we can choose ourselves.

My prayer for each of you as you read this - please look at your tarnishes and ask yourself – have I allowed Jesus in? Am I seeking Him daily? Have I allowed Him to know me and make me new?

I asked all of these questions over this last year going through this trial and many trials before. I didn't want to surrender. I wanted control. I wanted justice. I held unforgiveness in my heart. I survived so much trauma and I wanted to hold on to myself – to keep God, my Father, behind. I wanted to lead.

Journey to Eden

My sister, Aster, wrote a nine-month guided spiritual journey called "The Journey to Eden," which she invited me to attend at the peak of this court case. I attended and completed her spiritual journey from September 2024 to May 2025.

In this journey, I encountered Jesus in ways I never had before. The most celebrated expressions of Jesus's love for me were articulated in various spiritual exercises, imagery, discipleship, friendship, and prayer. This has empowered me to walk out in full surrender to Jesus, to stop looking back, to stop being triggered by Akuma's lack, and instead to look up and to trust Jesus the rest of the way.

My calling is to show the lost, broken, and hurting how to seek and find deliverance out of their own Egypt through my story and to help you find wholeness in Jesus alone. My prayer is that by sharing my story and standing with you in prayer, the encounter you have with Jesus will get Egypt out of you, as He did the same for me.

Pray continually and never give up. Seeds are transformed in the dark.
Stay rooted in Jesus, read His word, and surrender it all to Him.
Drop everything and run into His lap.
Full surrender brings abundant fruit.
Walk into His promises.
He is waiting for you…

You are fully known and loved by Jesus. He will hunt you down until you are found. He wants to do life with you.
"Let's spend our sunsets and sunrises together.
Every day – you and me."
- Jesus

My Encounter with Jesus

I ran up the mountain
in all of my desperation
screaming out to God

in agony

of all the pain that encompassed
my life

I ran until I reached the top
I knelt down in my deepest sorrow

and reached deep into the earth
picking up the grainy sand

clenching it into my hands
and releasing it as it blew away in the wind

I continued to scream out in agony
I cried and screamed into the skies above
as the sheer solitude of my pain drifted into the space
around me and echoed across that mountain top and
soaked into the valleys deep below

the clouds covered me
in various formations up above
the sun shone down on my back

my knees bent deep into the ground
the tears dripped from my cheeks
the sorrow
melted from my face

I continued to grip the earth and release it
as I wept the most sincere cry
deep within my being

suddenly, I felt warmth

a gentle stroke

up and down my spine

my body trembled
the pain of my life
affected my entire core
the pain was heavy, dense

the warm stroke continued

I turned and looked up

with blurry eyes
and stained cheeks covered in my pain
my blurry eyes met Jesus's face

His gaze comforted me
He looked so lovingly upon my face

He lifted me up

I wrapped my arms around Him
as tightly as I could

I clenched
onto His well-worn robe

He wrapped His arms around me

My body trembled as I held onto Him
with everything I had
as if my body collapsed into His
the pain was more than I could bear

the heaviness in my core intensified
my soul wept uncontrollably

He never let go
His arms wrapped me so wholly

I gently let my hands down by my side

I stepped back

Jesus stood there
His gaze upon me never wavered

I knew as soon as we stood there

with our gaze held on one another

He took the pain
I held
so deeply within

I could see how heavy the pain was
on Jesus

yet, His warmth never faded

I could see how much He loved me

The look in His eyes were deep, sincere
something I have never felt
something I couldn't grasp in that moment

Jesus wanted me to know
I was cherished
loved
His beloved daughter

He was so proud of me
for all the things I had done
He stood there
mesmerized by my beauty
He didn't see
what I saw

He lovingly looked upon me

I finally understood
the tears disappeared

He took me by the hand
twirled me around

He was captivated
by the woman I had transpired into
captivated by my strength
in all things I had overcome

He continued to twirl me by the hand
His gaze never fell from my face

He saw me for my beauty
not my ashes

we danced on the mountain top that day

no words spoken

eyes of love

eyes of understanding

the deepest love I had ever known

we sat down on the grassy hillside
He grabbed both of my hands
He placed them on his heart

He set my hands down
and wrapped His arm around my shoulder
He held onto me

we sat on that grassy hillside
and we looked at the valley
far below
the warm glowing sun
sat off in the distance away from us

it was beautiful
we sat speaking of everyday nothings,
laughing like old friends

His arm never left my side
He held onto me

we sat there together that day
Jesus and me

and finally, I felt free

I was free

I am free

Bibliography

Books Mentioned

A Parent's Guide to the Neonatal Intensive Care Unit. United States: Rocky Mountain Hospital for Children, 2008 – 2009.

Larson, Catherine Claire. Waiting in Wonder: Growing in Faith While You're Expecting: A Devotional Journal. Nashville: Thomas Nelson, 2013.

Moore, Beth. Breaking Free: The Journey, The Stories. Nashville: Lifeway Press, 1999. Revision 2009.

Terkeurst, Lysa. It's Not Supposed to Be This Way: Finding Unexpected Strength When Disappointments Leave You Shattered. Nashville: Nelson Books, 2018.

Websites and Companies Mentioned

Colorado Center for Reproductive Medicine (CCRM) Website, http://ccrmivf.com

Google Website, http://www.google.com

HCA Health ONE Presbyterian St. Luke's Hospital (PSL) Website, http://healthonecares.com/locations/presbyterian-st-lukes

HCA HealthONE Rocky Mountain Children's at Presbyterian St. Luke's Hospital Website, http://healthonecares.com/locations/rocky-mountain-childrens

Every Man's Battle In – Person Workshop Website, http://newlife.com/workshops/every-mans-battle/

Songs Mentioned

The Way by Pat Barrett
I Can Only Imagine by MercyMe
Baby Love by Nicole C. Mullins
Lord, I Need You by Chris Tomlin
Sovereign by Chris Tomlin
Every Praise by Hezekiah Walker

Movie Mentioned

I Can Only Imagine. Directed by Andrew Erwin and Jon Erwin, performances by Dennis Quaid and J. Michael Finley, LD Entertainment, March 16, 2018.

www.ingramcontent.com/pod-product-compliance
Lightning Source LLC
Chambersburg PA
CBHW020415130726
48053CB00020B/55

* 9 7 9 8 9 0 2 5 2 0 4 4 3 *